Get more
– *and more results* –
from your people

Alan Fowler

INSTITUTE OF PERSONNEL AND DEVELOPMENT

Typesetting by Wyvern 21, Bristol
and printed in Great Britain by
the Cromwell Press, Trowbridge, Wiltshire

British Library Cataloguing in Publication Data
A catalogue record for this book is available from the
British Library

ISBN 0-85292-748-7

IPD House, Camp Road, Wimbledon, London SW19 4UX
Tel: 0181-971-9000   Fax: 0181-263-3333
Registered office as above. Registered Charity No. 1038333
A company limited by guarantee. Registered in England No. 2931892

Get more
– *and more results* –
from your people

Alan Fowler has worked widely in both the private and public sectors, with personnel appointments in four industries and two local authorities. He is now a freelance consultant, a director of Personnel Publications Ltd, and a member of the editorial board of *People Management*, the fortnightly journal of the IPD. He writes extensively on personnel issues, with regular articles in *People Management* and the *Local Government Chronicle*. His books include *The Disciplinary Interview* (1996) and *Negotiating, Persuading and Influencing* (1995), both in the IPD's Management Shapers series; *Negotiation Skills and Strategies* (second edition 1996); *Redundancy* (1993); *Taking Charge: A guide to people management in today's public sector* (1993); and a companion volume to the present one, *Get More – and More Value – from Your People* (1998). All these titles are published by the IPD.

The Institute of Personnel and Development is the leading publisher of books and reports for personnel and training professionals, students, and all those concerned with the effective management and development of people at work. For details of all our titles, please contact the Publishing Department:

tel. 0181-263 3387

fax. 0181-263 3850

e-mail publish@ipd.co.uk

The catalogue of all IPD titles can be viewed on the IPD website:

http://www.ipd.co.uk

Contents

Foreword

All too often the glut of information that seems to come at us from every direction in this digital age is accompanied by a famine of wisdom. The field of managing and developing people is no exception. A bewildering range of books, learned journals, professional magazines, specialist bulletins, training packages and now on-line information services competes for our attention. It has become difficult even for the conscientious student to keep up-to-date with the latest thinking, and well-nigh impossible for the busy manager.

With so many authors appearing as guides to people management, a new role has become necessary – someone to act as a guide to the guides. A person specification might read as follows: someone with wide practical experience of every aspect of managing people, in several sectors and at both operational and strategic levels. Someone with the intellectual curiosity to search out new ideas and the analytical skills to put them in context. Someone who is in touch with a wide variety of HR and other managers, and knows their current concerns. And, perhaps most important, someone who has a talent for expression and loves to write.

Alan Fowler fits this specification in every respect. His formal studies included the one-year personnel management course at the London School of Economics in the 1950s, and an Open University degree in Social Sciences in the 1970s. His professional career included spells with Clarks Shoes, the Nigerian Sugar Company, Costain Construction, the Greater London Council and then Hampshire County Council, where he headed a combined personnel and management services department for ten years. In 1987 he was made a Companion of the former Institute of Personnel Management (now the IPD), and also became a freelance consultant. He has since worked with many different private- and public-sector clients. He has written a dozen books, many for the IPD, regularly contributes to *People Management* and *Local Government Chronicle*, teaches a diploma course and, until very recently, has been active as an employers'-side member on industrial tribunals.

He had already been contributing to *Personnel Management* magazine for many years before his monthly 'How To' series began. It was quickly apparent he had found his forte as the guide to the guides. Reader research and informal feedback showed 'How To' to be one of the most popular features of the magazine, so it was natural it should become a regular item in *People Management* (successor to *Personnel Management*) from its launch in 1995. Yet the principles and techniques Fowler describes so lucidly are of deep relevance to many besides HR and development professionals. His articles have now been collected into these two volumes, updated wherever necessary, providing a rich seam of material to this wider readership.

Rob MacLachlan, Editor, *People Management*

Introduction

Effective management of people lies at the heart of all major corporate initiatives. It is easy for directors to issue edicts that their companies must become more customer-focused, more quality-conscious or genuinely open to talent from all backgrounds, any of which can indeed make the difference between success and failure in the marketplace. Yet exhortation is never enough. If I have learned one thing from my long experience as a practitioner and consultant, it is that these inspiring ideals become realities only when employers find ways to:

- create a supportive corporate climate
- recruit people who possess – or can rapidly acquire – appropriate competencies
- communicate the key messages, in concrete practical terms, to all employees
- build strong teams, set challenging objectives and constantly monitor progress against targets
- reward the right behaviour while discouraging – and, where necessary, disciplining – 'wrong-doing'
- provide focused and cost-effective training in the key skills

cope constructively with conflict without demotivating staff.

Taken on its own, it might not seem to matter much if staff returning from sick leave are treated as malingerers, if a major health and safety initiative is misspelled, dog-eared and tacked up on an untidy notice-board, or if a company car scheme makes half the managers feel under-valued. Yet the cumulative impact of such policies (or lack of policy) will be an environment in which commitment and enthusiasm never flourish. Only people can add essential value to an organisation's inanimate resources of money, equipment, material and information. Effective employers realise this and so devote much of their time and energy to maximising this contribution. In the long term, even the tiniest details of a payment system or an appraisal scheme will make a real impact on how people behave. And that is why I firmly believe employers should always pursue best practice in people management, whether or not they use the services of a dedicated personnel department or expert.

Together with its companion volume, *Get More – and More Value – from Your People,* this book brings together 50 articles that I originally wrote for the IPD's fortnightly magazine *People Management* (or its predecessors *Personnel Management* and *PM Plus*). All have stood the test of time and remain highly relevant today, although they have been updated where necessary to take account of recent legal or other environmental changes. (Most sections also include useful addresses and/or details of books by the IPD or other publishers for readers who wish to pursue individual topics in greater depth.) Each formed part of a long-running and continuing series of 'how to' pieces designed to provide quick reference guides to good practice across the full range of people management techniques. I have been delighted by their popularity with both HR students and professionals, although the key messages are equally essential for line managers in smaller or devolved organisations who have day-to-day responsibility for many aspects of people management.

This volume provides important insights for anyone involved in communicating with employees, enhancing their performance or dealing with disputes. It explores how employers can create a culture that truly supports customer care, safe working practices and equal opportunities, and looks at the best means of offering personnel support. Developing a positive corporate climate, ensuring everyone is well-informed, building high-achieving teams and coping with inevitable conflicts – these represent at least half the spectrum of essential people management skills. They are not, of course, the whole story – hence the need for a companion volume. But any organisation that takes on board the key lessons about the 25 topics covered here will have gone a long way towards getting more – and more results – from its people.

Creating the
right climate

1   Organisational culture

The concept of organisational culture is one of the most powerful influences on the way organisations perceive themselves and make decisions about their structure and style. There has always been some recognition that employees' attitudes and behaviour are influenced by the characteristics of the organisation they work for, but the idea that a planned programme of management action can shape or change this cultural environment is, in historical terms, relatively new.

There are many definitions of culture, ranging from the simple 'the way we do things around here' to lengthy sociological descriptions which tend to emphasise attitudinal rather than behavioural factors. For practical purposes a conceptual framework is needed which goes beyond the simple definition but describes cultural characteristics in terms which refer directly to everyday organisational experience. In this chapter, culture is taken to be an amalgam of the effect on employee attitudes, behaviour and effectiveness of

- values (the qualities and characteristics the organisation considers important)

- structures (how work and employees are differentiated and grouped)
- systems and procedures (how work is done and conduct regulated)
- style (particularly how managers behave)
- customs (the informal practices that develop over time)
- beliefs and myths (the ideas and stories that grow up about the organisation).

The informal aspects of culture – the habits and attitudes which develop over time – can be more powerful than any formal attempt to change them unless this action is well-planned and comprehensive. An attempt to change culture by altering the organisational structure while leaving values undefined and systems unaltered may do little more than reinforce employees' existing mythology about top management's moving the chairs on the deck of the *Titanic*. All the cultural elements interact, and all must be considered in planning for change.

A cultural analysis

It is impossible to plan an effective change programme without first defining what cultural change aims to achieve and how this differs from the existing situation. The objective of many organisations in managing cultural change is to move from a static or rigid culture to one that is flexible and adaptable. Another is to develop a customer-oriented organisation.

A cultural analysis can be undertaken to identify the current characteristics that are blocking progress towards the targeted result of the change programme. This might consist, for example, of a schedule of the contrasting features of static and adaptable cultures, scoring the current state of the organisation on a scale between these two extremes. Such a schedule of contrasting features may comprise 30 or more characteristics, and the precise details need to reflect the particular features of each situation. If the prime need is to develop a customer-oriented culture, the list should include items specific to that objective.

The results of such an analysis should indicate where the main emphasis needs to be placed in designing a change programme. It may suggest, for example, that existing structures are suitable for flexibility in decision-making but centralised systems are inhibiting this from being achieved, and that flexibility has never been positively promoted as a core value.

Outline programme

Assuming that much more needs to be done than any simple adjustment to one element, the next step is to design an outline programme that identifies all the main components and stages. Deciding the right order in which the various parts of the programme are to be implemented is a vital part of this design process. There may be particular circumstances in which a different sequence is needed, but the following schedule has often been found to be effective:

- Top management determines the objectives of the programme in the form of a mission statement, and is seen throughout the organisation to give this their total commitment. Without genuine and committed top management support the change programme will almost certainly fail.

- A senior manager is given responsibility for the overall management and co-ordination of the programme as a major project, with a project budget.
- The messages about the need for change (and what the change aims to achieve) are explained and promoted throughout the organisation. The first stage in this awareness or marketing exercise should involve all managers at all levels. The extent to which managers understand and become enthusiastic about the programme will largely determine its outcome. The second stage in the awareness programme is to extend it to the whole workforce – an activity in which all managers must play an important role through their formal and informal briefings and explanations to their staff.
- If structural and systems changes are involved, they are implemented as closely as possible in time. New structures will not be effective until supporting procedures are in place. New procedures need to reflect new roles within the new structure.
- Training is needed to help managers and staff develop new skills, and to demonstrate to employees that the organisation is committed to change. It will give positive help to employees in adapting to new values, roles, and systems.
- Appraisal and reward systems are reviewed and revised to ensure that the influences they have on employees' perception of what is important reinforce the targeted new cultural characteristics.

Thought is given to the use of symbols (such as a new logo) and special events or external recognition (such as ISO 9000, trade awards and Investors in People) to stimulate interest, emphasise the organisation's new qualities and generate pride in achievement.

Throughout the programme full use is made of consultative machinery to enable employees, through their trade unions or other elected representatives, to contribute ideas and suggestions to the process, and to resolve any problems which may arise.

The personnel contribution

It is important that the purpose and programme of change is seen throughout the organisation as driven and owned by the executive management, and not as a scheme promoted by the personnel department. Nevertheless, because organisational culture has a strong human resource component in terms of attitudes, skills and behaviour, the personnel manager has a vital role to play in any change programme. In addition to being a member of the corporate management team, with a particular contribution to make to the strategic redesign of organisation structures, the personnel manager should address employee communications, new training needs, the design and implementation of any new appraisal and reward systems, and the monitoring of attitudinal change.

Existing employee communications will probably prove inadequate for the volume and intensity of information needed to generate interest and commitment throughout the workforce. Additional measures may include special staff bulletins, poster campaigns, scripted briefing notes for managers to ensure consistency of the message, employee focus groups and mass staff meetings addressed by top management.

Early attention needs to be given to the identification of new skills involved in the operation of new structures and systems. Many programmes of cultural change include the devolution of decision-making and the empowerment of front-line employees. This can generate significant training needs, as can the introduction of an internal market culture – a common theme in much of the public sector.

It is essential that the style of training fits the desired style of the organisation, and that its link with other elements in the programme is clearly indicated. Tailor-made in-house training, though with the assistance of an external facilitator, has often proved the best approach.

Many cultural change programmes are intended to have a qualitative impact – for example, to develop quality consciousness. It is essential that such objectives are reflected in any systems of performance management, appraisal and reward. A target-based scheme of performance-related pay carries powerful messages about the things the organisation considers important, and unless these targets are linked directly to the newly defined values, the scheme may operate in direct conflict with the aims of the change programme. A very thorough analysis of the whole appraisal and reward system and its redesign to support the desired changes in attitude and priorities may be one of the main keys to the success of the programme.

Achieving real cultural change goes much deeper than

the apparently successful operation of new structures and systems. Fundamentally, it is concerned with changing how people feel and act, so trends in employees' views and attitudes need to be monitored and the results fed back into the programme as it develops. It may take several years for major changes to become a normal and accepted way of organisational life, and feedback from annual attitude surveys can be valuable indicators of the rate of success and of aspects to which more emphasis may need to be given.

Further information

1 WILLIAMS A., DOBSON P. *and* WALTERS M. *Changing Culture: New organisational approaches.* 2nd edn. London, Institute of Personnel Management, 1993.

2 WALTERS M. *Employee Attitude and Opinion Surveys.* 2nd edn. London, Institute of Personnel and Development, 1996.

2 Monitoring equal opportunities

Most organisations claim to operate equal opportunities policies, and many have published statements to this effect. Yet systematic monitoring to assess the effectiveness of these policies is by no means universal. Some employers think the issue only concerns keeping records of employees' ethnic origins and consider that doing this would cause problems with the workforce or with job applicants. Those who think this way are overlooking three issues.

Firstly, equal opportunities monitoring is no different in principle from any other form of managerial monitoring. It is poor management practice to introduce any policy with no way of assessing whether it is effective. Secondly, a sound equal opportunities policy should aim to eliminate adverse discrimination of all kinds, whether or not that is required by law. So an effective monitoring system should cover factors such as age or accent as well as the statutory factors of sex, race, disability – and, in Northern Ireland, religion. Ethnic monitoring is only one element in a comprehensive personnel system.

Thirdly, monitoring – including ethnic monitoring – has been introduced by many major private and public sector organisations without any adverse reaction from existing employees.

Although there are far more positive reasons for monitoring than simply to avoid legal difficulties, it should be noted that employment tribunals hearing complaints of unlawful discrimination (in recruitment or promotion, for example) expect the employer to provide evidence of the numbers of applicants and employees of each gender and ethnic category. Inability to do so can cast doubt on the claim to be an equal opportunity employer and undermine any defence against claims of discrimination.

Basic records

There are two aspects to monitoring which apply to all forms of equal opportunities: ensuring that basic records of applicants and employees include the necessary information, and using this information to produce statistics which indicate how well the equal opportunies policy is working.

Few organisations, if any, should have difficulty in keeping gender records because conventional record systems have always distinguished men from women. The requirement to record registered disabled persons – repealed by the 1995 Disability Discrimination Act – also made at least this limited form of disability recording a normal feature. While this Act does not require records to be kept, it is difficult to see how any organisation will know how well it is complying with the legislation unless some documentation is kept on applicants and employees who have disabilities. The Employers' Forum on Disability suggests that the two most useful questions are

- Do you consider yourself to have a disability?
- Do you feel your disability could limit your career prospects?

If versions of these questions are used in application forms, they are probably best supplemented by a third question which asks for brief details of the disability concerned.

In recruitment and internal promotions, the reasons for non-selection of all applicants, both at the interview and final selection stages, should be recorded. A possible form of categorisation might be:

for applicants not selected for interview:
- inadequate details provided
- insufficient relevant experience
- inadequate qualifications
- other reasons (specified).

for candidates interviewed but not selected:
- experience less suited than appointee's
- less qualified than appointee
- less skilled/competent than appointee
- personality less suited than appointee's.

For unsuccessful disabled applicants, in addition to the reasons listed above, it may be advisable to record whether the reason for rejection was the impracticability of making reasonable adjustments to working arrangements for an otherwise suitable candidate.

Records of ethnic origin

Organisations introducing ethnic monitoring have two main decisions to make: which system of ethnic classification to use, and how to collect this information. The Commission for Racial Equality recommends the nine categories used in the 1991 national census:

White
Black – African
Black – Caribbean
Black – other (please specify)
Indian
Pakistani
Bangladeshi
Chinese
Other (please specify).

However, there is no legal requirement to use these particular categories and some organisations separate those of EU from those of non-EU origin, or include further Irish or Arab categories. There are also mixed views about using colour as the main distinguishing factor, although if it is considered important, one classification in use by some organisations is:

Black/Afro-Caribbean
Black/Asian
Black/UK
Black/Other
White/UK
White/Other European
White/Other.

The precise classification should depend in part on any

local characteristics which might result in a localised form of discrimination (eg against a large local Irish community). It may also be influenced by the data collection methods used. For job applicants this has to be done by self-classification, either in a section of the application form or on a separate equal opportunity monitoring questionnaire. Until such time as the collection of ethnic information is considered normal practice, it is advisable to give applicants a statement of the reason for such questions and supply notes which explain what is meant by ethnic origin and the various ethnic categories.

Because of possible misunderstanding or suspicion, some organisations use a questionnaire separate from the application form and preface it with a statement along the following lines:

> We operate a policy of equal opportunity and wish to ensure that all applicants are considered solely on their merits. So we need to be able to check that decisions are not influenced by unfair or unlawful discrimination. To help us do this we would be grateful if you would complete this short questionnaire. Your answers will be treated in the utmost confidence and will be used only for statistical purposes.

The questionnaire might include a section on disability. Some organisations also include questions about marital and parental status – with a note that legislation bans discrimination on such grounds – because it may be helpful to have data on these factors to rebut any unfounded allegation of bias against, say, single mothers with young children.

The section on ethnic origin might begin: 'I would

describe my cultural or ethnic origin as . . . (please tick the appropriate box).' A note is needed to make clear that ethnic origin is not a matter of nationality, right of abode in the UK or place of birth.

Eventually ethnic data collected during recruitment will provide the data for the whole workforce, but as this may take decades to accumulate, a campaign is also needed to obtain ethnic records for existing employees. There are three main methods of obtaining this information:

- self-classification, using the same type of questionnaire as for applicants
- managerial/supervisory categorisation, by observation
- classification by discussion with each employee.

Each method has advantages and disadvantages. Self-classification reduces suspicion and should be accurate. Its main disadvantage is that because it is voluntary the response rate may be too low to be of any use. Some organisations have experienced responses as low as 30 per cent. Classification by managers' or supervisors' observation can be organised to obtain 100 per cent coverage but may have to use a very crude and colour-based system (eg White; Black African; Black Asian; Other). It may also generate suspicion and fear about what is being recorded.

Classification by discussion with each employee is the most reliable and generally acceptable method, although it may be time-consuming. Managers, or personnel officers, see each employee, explain the purpose of the exercise, and agree their ethnic classification. The disadvantage in an organisation of any size is the time it takes to talk to each and every employee. One way of reducing the time involved is to begin with a self-classification exercise and then use classification by discussion only with those employees who fail to return the initial questionnaire.

Whichever method is used, it is essential to explain fully the purpose of the exercise and tell employees how the data will be used. In a unionised environment the first step should be consultation with the trade unions. The whole process will be eased if it can be launched as an agreed action. Explanations and assurances need also to be given to employees individually – an essential point if union representation is weak or non-existent. A written note is inadequate. Some employees are likely to have views or fears which require discussion, and this highlights the importance of adequate briefing of managers and supervisors. It is vital that supervisory staff are able to answer questions from their employees and do not give the impression that they either do not understand or, worse, oppose the scheme. The personnel department can act as long-stop to handle any really difficult issues, but it is for line managers to deal constructively with most employee queries.

Monitoring

Once the basic data is recorded, consideration can be given to the form which actual monitoring is to take. Essentially this consists of analysis of, first, the results of all decisions where discrimination might occur, showing numbers and percentages of persons by gender, disability, age and ethnic origin. The decisions concerned may include

- rejections before interview
- rejections after interview

- appointments
- promotions
- training course attendances
- grievance cases
- disciplinary cases.

There should also be periodic reviews of the characteristics of the whole workforce, analysed by the various equal opportunity categories, separately for each employee category (manual, non-manual, etc), grade or salary level, hierarchical/managerial level and department. The format of such statistics should be standardised so that periodic (often annual) analyses show not just each year's figures but also trends. Is the number of women in senior grades increasing or decreasing? Are more black people applying for jobs, or being promoted? Are more older people being selected for interview? An organisation which cannot answer such important and practical questions is in no position to claim it is an equal opportunities employer.

Further information

1 Codes of practice published by the Equal Opportunities Commission and the Commission for Racial Equality, and the statutory codes on disability.

2 CLARKE L. *Discrimination.* 2nd edn. London, Institute of Personnel and Development, 1995.

3 KANDOLA R. *and* FULLERTON J. *Diversity in Action: Managing the mosaic.* 2nd edn. London, Institute of Personnel and Development, 1998.

4 PEARN KANDOLA. *Tools for Managing Diversity.* London, Institute of Personnel and Development, 1998.

3   Health and safety policies

The production of formal policy statements for most aspects of employment is a matter of choice, not a statutory requirement. Most personnel managers hold the view that written policies serve a valuable purpose by committing the employer to maintain specified standards and ensuring that this commitment is supported throughout the organisation. However, policy statements that are not reflected in day-to-day management practice generate cynicism in the workforce. Very detailed statements, particularly those which confuse procedures with policies, may also restrict an organisation's operational flexibility. In recent years there has been a trend towards simpler statements of core employment values. This, on the other hand, will not serve in relation to health and safety, for which written policies are required by statute.

The basic legal requirement is in the Health and Safety at Work Act 1974 and applies to all undertakings with five or more employees. The Act states that every employer must prepare – and revise as necessary – a written statement of general policy towards the health and safety of their employees. The key features of this statutory provision are: the policy statement must be in writing and must be kept up-to-date; it must explain how the policy is implemented; and all employees must be kept informed. The existence or absence of a written statement can be used in evidence if an employer is prosecuted under the Act, and individual managers as well as the corporate employer are open to prosecution. Although the Act gives no further details about the content of the policy statement, the Health and Safety Executive has issued guidance which emphasises that the statement should at least set out the various responsibilities for health and safety.

In the 25 years since the Health and Safety at Work Act, some employers may have become lax about the issue and the revision of safety policy statements, or may have produced only the barest minimum of statements which do little to maintain a high standard of safety awareness among managers and employees. What has had more impact in some cases than the requirement for a policy statement has been a wave of safety regulations on specific topics, most of which have originated in EC directives. These regulations do not amend the 1974 policy requirement, but they do prescribe a number of additional matters for which employers have to maintain a written record – such as safety checks on pressure vessels, and general risk assessments. It is open to employers to include these items in the policy statement or append them, and many employers have decided that this is a sensible way to meet these new provisions.

The requirements of most general relevance are in the

Management of Health and Safety at Work Regulations 1992. They are supplemented by a Health and Safety Commission Code of Practice which, while not itself legally enforceable, may be used in court proceedings to indicate whether or not an employer has complied with the statutory regulations.

Information to record

The matters which employers are required to record, and to which reference may therefore be included in (or attached to) the policy statement, are:

- the findings of risk assessment
- details of arrangements for the effective planning, organisation, control, monitoring and review of preventive and protective health and safety measures
- details of competent persons appointed to assist the employer in implementing the safety policy
- procedures to be followed in the event of serious and imminent danger (such as fires or bombs).

The regulations require the employer to provide employees with comprehensible and relevant information on any health and safety risks, and on preventive measures. Employers must also consult their employees' safety representatives about the provision of health and safety information required by law. Not everything which employers must record or notify employees of is appropriate for inclusion in the policy statement. Detailed information specific to particular groups of employees is best provided direct to those concerned. Information subject to frequent change may need also to be recorded or notified separately from the policy, although it is important that the statement is reviewed regularly.

The structure of a safety policy statement

The suggested structure of a policy statement includes:

- a short opening section which sets out the organisation's commitments to health and safety
- a section describing managers' and employees' safety responsibilities, including the arrangements for competent persons
- a description of the way the organisation plans, monitors and reviews its health and safety activities
- an explanation of possible risks and the preventive measures in place, including the procedures for dealing with emergencies
- a description of the consultative arrangements with the trade unions' safety representatives.

Because legislation requires all employers to meet detailed statutory health and safety requirements, some may argue there is little point in an opening section which states the employer's commitment to complying with the law. However, individual managers and the workforce at large may not believe the employer really intends to take the subjects seriously unless there is a well-publicised statement to this effect. The policy can also do more than simply state an intention to meet all legal requirements. It can emphasise the importance to the business of reducing accident and sickness rates; it may draw attention to the need to protect the environment against the consequences of accidents; it can refer to the benefits to employees of their co-operation in securing a safe working environment.

Who is responsible?

If the organisation has a mission statement and has publicised its core values, the opening section of the health and safety policy can be cross-referenced to show the link between it and the overall culture and aims of the business. The section of the policy statement that covers responsibilities should set out who is responsible for overall health and safety standards and for specific safety tasks. It should make it clear that the chief executive and board (or the public-sector equivalent) carry ultimate responsibility, but that the duty to ensure safe working also falls individually on every manager and supervisor in each of their workplaces. Specialist and advisory appointments should be identified and their responsibilities outlined. This applies to professional safety officers, together with occupational health staff and the organisation's medical adviser or nurse.

Information should be given in this section about the appointment of competent persons. Competent persons do not have to be qualified but they must have sufficient knowledge of current health and safety practice relevant to the particular work involved. They need not be employees. The statement should explain the organisation's policy on this point and outline the competent persons' responsibilities. This part of the statement should end with an explanation of the responsibilities of individual employees, which include duties under the 1992 regulations to report hazards or any shortfall in the employer's preventive measures.

The management of health and safety

The statement should also outline the way the organisation manages its health and safety activities. The emphasis here is on procedures, and may include:

- a commitment for the board to consider periodic health and safety reports
- a requirement for departments or other units to supplement the organisation's policy statement with local statements
- the inclusion of health and safety as a factor to examine when acquiring new materials or equipment
- arrangements for periodic reviews, both of health and safety standards and of the policy itself
- a commitment to provide adequate training, particularly for new recruits: the 1992 regulations make training a statutory requirement, and the policy statement needs to outline how this is to be met.

Other matters for inclusion

Detailed records of risk assessments cannot be included in a standing policy statement, although the procedure to be followed in making these assessments can. Records of inspections and consequent action should be kept by the managers of the particular departments or units involved. This responsibility can be noted in the section of the policy dealing with safety arrangements. However, any type of safety risk common to the whole organisation can be included as a section within or as a supplement to the policy statement. When assessing risks it is also necessary to consider their relevance to visitors, the public and subcontractors as well as to employees. The policy statement should acknowledge the organisation's responsibilities in this respect.

The only form of consultation prescribed by statute is with the safety representatives appointed or elected by the organisation's recognised trade unions. Many organisations, however, include health and safety issues within the remit of their joint consultative arrangements, whether or not the employee representatives are trade union members. It is therefore helpful for the policy statement to set out the nature and purpose of any relevant consultative systems. The policy statement itself should also be the subject of consultation, not least because one of its objectives should be to secure employee commitment to its objectives.

Further information

1 HEALTH AND SAFETY COMMISSION. *Writing a Safety Policy Statement*. London, Health and Safety Commission.

2 HEALTH AND SAFETY COMMISSION. *Code of Practice: Management of health and safety at work*. London, Health and Safety Commission.

4   Customer care

Customer care is widely recognised as a high priority for both private- and public-sector organisations. Successful firms have always recognised the importance of a reputation for excellence in their service to customers, and in the last two decades this view been translated into programmes of action by all but a minority of companies.

However, this action is not always fully effective. Some organisations have done little more than publicise customer care slogans and give their front-line staff superficial charm school training, thus succeeding only in raising – and then failing to meet – their customers' expectations. A successful customer care policy requires a comprehensive action plan, together with commitment at the top of the organisation and a declaration by senior management of the purpose of the policy and their determination to see it succeed. This is a matter of vision – not something which can be delegated to middle management or of concern only to those employees in direct contact with the customers. Top management involvement does not cease with endorsing a vision statement or policy document. It must be seen to continue throughout the programme and beyond.

To implement a customer care action plan or campaign, a project leader should be appointed to co-ordinate and monitor the programme, perhaps with a small project team drawn from various parts of the organisation to guarantee a range of know-how and internal contacts. The project leader must be seen to have the active backing of top management to ensure the programme is perceived by the whole organisation as an activity of major importance. Cynicism is probably the biggest single threat to a campaign's success and will emerge immediately staff gain any impression that the policy lacks top management commitment or is merely public window-dressing.

An audit of current standards is an essential precursor to the design of the eventual action plan. Managerial assumptions about how well customers are currently served are often very wide of the mark. There are two main sources of information to be tapped at this stage: customers and the organisation's own employees. It is also helpful to research the customer care standards and practices of competitors. Customer research may include:

- personal interviews of customers by senior management, seeking views about current standards
- questionnaires to customers along similar lines
- analyses of customer complaints
- senior managers' taking spells of duty on reception or inquiry desks to experience direct customer contact
- for public-sector bodies, such as local and health authorities, public opinion surveys commissioned from specialist consultancies.

The best methods to use vary with the nature and size of the customer base. For a company with a relatively small number of major customers, the personal approach is generally the most productive. At the other end of the scale are public bodies whose 'customers' are the population at large. Opinion surveys, designed by professionals to ensure representative sampling, may then be the main source of data.

The organisation's own employees – particularly those in direct contact with customers – are a rich source of information and ideas. They are the people to whom customers first complain if things go wrong. Employees may be involved directly in customer research by establishing customer care teams charged with examining specific aspects of the organisation's activities and reporting their findings and proposals to senior management.

Staff at large can also be asked to submit comments and suggestions on how customer care might be improved. Questions to stimulate ideas can be along the lines: 'If you were a customer, what would you think were the good and bad points of how you are treated by the company?' Prizes can be awarded for the best ideas.

Once a full picture has been obtained of the current standard of customer service, together with ideas for improvement, a set of action plans can be developed. The objectives of these plans need to be clearly identified – a generalised policy of serving customers better is not enough, nor is an *ad hoc* selection of those suggestions which appear easiest or least costly to implement. Wherever possible, measurable targets are needed so that later progress can be monitored. These targets should be set within a policy framework that indicates which aspects of customer care have the highest priority.

It may be helpful to group the various elements of the

programme into three categories. The first comprises physical factors, such as access to buildings, signs and logos, the design and quality of the product, and the availability of spare parts, packaging and delivery.

The second category – procedural factors – would include the design of relevant documents, the routing of customer inquiries, ordering and invoicing systems, and complaints procedures. This may also need to include significant changes to the way jobs are structured – for example, to devolve more decision-making authority to front-line staff.

Finally, there are personal factors, such as the way reception and telephone staff greet and relate to customers, the attitudes all staff should display towards meeting customer requirements, and the response to customer requests.

The action plans need also to include the design of the next stage: internal publicity and training. The personnel function has a particularly important role in this stage, concerned with explaining the new customer care message, gaining employee commitment and enthusiasm, and training in new skills. Initial interest should have been stimulated by the earlier phase in which employees were asked for their views and suggestions. Now the organisation's task is to publicise and explain the full plan of action.

Those organisations which have achieved a major improvement in customer care have all found it essential to give the programme an extremely high profile. Employees' attention and interest has to be secured right at the start, and this needs a lively launch and a widely publicised campaign. It may be reinforced by adopting a campaign logo and simple slogan which is then used on all the training and information material.

The ideal launch, if logistics permit, is a mass event attended by all employees, addressed by top management and including professionally produced visual material such as a video or similar presentation which dramatises the need for change. The message of the launch needs evoking throughout the course of the campaign, and publicity material such as posters and a campaign news-sheet can play a useful part.

Specific training in customer care is another essential element of the campaign. It may need to cover several different aspects:

- training for reception and 'first-contact' staff in how to display a helpful and welcoming manner
- training in any new systems being introduced to improve customer care, such as a quicker order and delivery procedure
- development training to help those staff who have been given more decision-making authority
- general customer awareness courses for staff at all levels across the whole organisation
- secondments of individual staff to work for short periods for major customers – thus developing an ability to see things from the customers' viewpoint
- visits of staff to other organisations which have a reputation for high customer care standards.

The initial impact of a customer care campaign can fade rapidly unless a permanent monitoring system is put in place and its results given high-level management attention. Everyone must be kept aware of the priority the organisation places on customer service: top management needs a reporting system which enables trends to be identified so that failings can be corrected and successes recognised and rewarded.

Performance indicators, which should be linked with performance and quality management systems and appraisal schemes, are an important monitoring device. The ratio of the number of complaints to the number of transactions, the cost of supplying replacement items, and achievement against charter targets are examples of such indicators. Other monitoring systems include complaint analyses which go beyond simple statistics to show the nature, causes and trends of customer dissatisfaction. Customer opinion surveys carried out at regular intervals are particularly valuable in revealing trends in general customer satisfaction.

Finally, monitoring can be done through service inspections, such as unannounced management visits to front-line units, service testing by 'mystery shoppers', anonymous telephone queries, and visits to major customers to discuss their views on service standards. It is important for monitoring not to be seen by staff as concentrating on fault-finding. Improvements in customer care should be identified and publicised: those responsible should be given recognition and, if appropriate, some tangible reward. Customers, too, should be encouraged to comment on good service so staff can see that their efforts have not gone unnoticed.

Further information

BEE F. *and* R. *Customer Care.* London, Institute of Personnel and Development, 1995.

Changing places

5   Relocation

There can be many reasons for changing an organisation's location. The existing premises may have been outgrown, overheads might be reduced by moving to a lower-cost area, or it may be an advantage to move closer to major customers.

Any relocation involves considerable logistical problems in both maintaining continuity of operational activity and handling the physical move. But the issue that can cause lasting damage if mishandled is the reaction of employees, success or failure depending primarily on the extent to which they are willing to relocate.

For organisations based in several locations, a related issue is the need from time to time for individual employees to transfer from one site to another. Reluctance to move may conflict with the organisation's staffing plans, so measures which ease employees' relocation problems become a necessary feature of personnel policy and practice.

There is much more to successful relocation than providing financial assistance. All the following issues need to be addressed:

- the contractual position
- employee and trade union consultation

- employee and family visits to the new location
- the impact on the education of employees' children
- partners' employment
- employees' housing needs and problems
- employees' removal arrangements and costs.

The contractual position

It is important to be clear whether employees are contractually bound to accept a change of location. Some organisations include a mobility clause in their contractual terms to the effect that 'You may be required to work at any location the company specifies.' In such cases a refusal to move might justify dismissal, although the courts may well not support the enforcement of an unreasonable mobility requirement.

In the more common situation in which there are no formal mobility obligations, a major location change would normally be interpreted as being outside the employment contract and so liable to produce an entitlement to redundancy payments for employees who reasonably refuse to relocate. Whether a refusal is reasonable has to be decided on a case-by-case basis, taking the employee's personal circumstances into account.

This is not to suggest that relocation should be handled as a legal process, but in costing a relocation plan it is very necessary to consider the possible scale of redundancy payments to employees who may not agree, or be able, to move.

Consultation

Without effective information and consultation, rumours about a major relocation will spread rapidly, morale will drop, and there will be a serious risk of losing key employees. Two kinds of information channel are desirable.

The first is to set up briefing groups throughout the organisation, supplying all managers with full and continuously updated information to relay to their staff about the move.

The second method is to have a special joint consultative group of trade union or other employee representatives who meet frequently with the managers responsible for planning the move. This can go beyond a simple information forum and involve employee representatives in the planning process – for example, by contributing proposals for the layout of workstations in the new premises.

Visits to the new location

Willingness to relocate is influenced mainly by factors unrelated to the workplace. Many staff are for example likely to have ill-informed impressions of the area which they are being asked to move to. Mental images in the south of a cold and grimy north, and in the north of an expensive and unfriendly south, are still common.

Many questions need to be answered. What are the leisure facilities in the new area? What is its public transport network like? What are the shops like? Where are the schools and hospitals?

One way of dealing with this is to issue a fact file with information to answer all probable general questions. This may consist of documentation produced in-house and of leaflets and other material obtained from such bodies as the local authority in the new area. Many councils publish booklets describing their area and listing the various amenities. Fact files for each of the company's locations can also be held for issue when needed by individual transferees.

Where a major location change is planned, another approach is to commission a video of the principal features of the new area and work site for showing at staff meetings. This can bring the area to life in a way that documentation cannot. If budgets permit, copies of the video can be made available for employees to borrow for home viewing.

But neither of these measures is a satisfactory substitute for visits. Coach tours of the area, with free time for employees and their families to explore the place on their own, can be particularly valuable in combating fears about a major relocation.

The involvement of family members in these visits is essential because initial family resistance to moving can be a much stronger influence on an employee's decision than anything related to work. Additional visits of work groups of employees to the actual workplace – with full information about facilities such as catering, travel-to-work facilities and car parking – can do much to meet the many concerns which may otherwise result in reluctance or refusal to move.

Employees can also be given financial assistance in making visits to new locations, particularly for house-hunting. It is common practice to pay travel costs for a set number of visits and to contribute towards the costs of an employee's living away from and visiting home, for any period after the transfer but before the purchase of a new home has been completed.

Children's education

An issue of much concern to parents is the risk that relocation might disrupt their children's education, particularly at O-level and A-level grades.

For young children the main question may be the accessibility of suitable schools. In the case of single or small numbers of employees it may be sufficient to provide lists of schools and advice on contacting the head teachers. For larger numbers it may be possible to arrange for a representative of the local education authority to meet groups of parents.

Partners' employment

For many employees, relocation will disrupt the employment of a spouse (or a working-age child). This may well be the deciding issue for staff who are not willing to impose such a change on their partners or to live away from home. In other cases employees will be willing to move if their partners can get a job in the new area. The employer may be able to help by giving priority to employees' family members when filling suitable vacancies at the new location or by liaising with employment agencies in the new area so that family members can be put in touch with potential employers.

Housing

For many employees the biggest single issue will be housing. The two dominant questions are: 'Will I be able to sell my present home, and for how much?' and 'Will I be able to find a new home, in the right place, at a price I can afford?'

Supplementary questions will relate to timescales,

bridging loans and the costs of solicitors and estate agents. Moving home has long been recognised as a highly stressful experience, and employees need every possible assistance if this issue is not to prove the biggest single factor that prevents acceptance of relocation.

A certain amount can be done by the employer in purely financial terms, particularly through the payment of professional fees and the costs of bridging loans. Additionally, if the new area has higher housing costs some form of subsidy of the additional mortgage payments, scaled down over a period of, say, five years, may be considered. Similar financial assistance may also be needed to meet any significant shortfall between the outstanding mortgage and the selling price of the existing house.

But payments of these kinds do not go to the heart of the problem, which is usually the hassle, uncertainty and delays involved in the actual selling and buying process. It is for this reason that specialist relocation companies are increasingly being used to handle every aspect of the process.

Although details vary, the typical transaction involves the relocation company's getting two or three independent valuations of the employee's current property and agreeing a guaranteed value, the figure varying according to whether it is on a quick sale basis to avoid bridging costs or on an open market basis.

The relocation company then takes control of the sale, at the same time releasing the agreed sum in order that the employee can proceed without delay to a purchase at the new location. From the employee's viewpoint the relocation company acts as a chain-breaker (or chain-preventer) and takes away all the hassle of dealing with solicitors, buyers, insurance on the property if it has to stand empty, bridging loans and the like. For the employer, although there are obviously costs, it goes a long way towards ensuring acceptance of the relocation and a motivated workforce whose commitment is not eroded by the disruption and nagging worry of unsold properties or separation from family life.

Removal costs

Some relocation companies include information and assistance with furniture removal as part of a comprehensive service. Otherwise, it is normal for employees to be asked to obtain two or three quotations from reputable removal firms (their names can be provided in the general information pack); the lowest quote is then accepted and paid for by the employer.

In addition, it is normal to pay some form of disturbance allowance as a contribution to the costs of such items as new curtains and floor coverings. To ensure that any such payment is made free of tax it is advisable to obtain copies of receipts. The Inland Revenue is emphatic that the concession to make payments tax-free is available only when the payments are reimbursements of expenses and not a generalised benefit.

Further information

1 SHORTLAND S. *Relocation: A practical guide.* London, Institute of Personnel Management, 1990.
2 Association of Relocation Agents: 11 Marlborough Place, Brighton, BN1 1UB (01273 624455).
3 CBI Employee Relocation Council: Centre Point, Oxford Street, London, WC1A 1DU (0171 379 7400).

6   Transfer of undertakings

Although the Transfer of Undertakings (Protection of Employment) Regulations – commonly known as Tupe – date back to 1981, uncertainties about their interpretation have still not been wholly resolved. The two main difficulties have been a lack of clarity in the legal definition of 'undertakings' and 'transfers', and the extent to which the regulations apply to the contracting out of individual functions previously undertaken in-house – as distinct from the transfer of a complete business. This remains a major issue for the public sector as a result of market testing and compulsory competitive tendering (CCT) and a general growth in outsourcing.

As drafted initially, the regulations applied only to undertakings in the nature of commercial ventures, thus excluding the public sector. Decisions of the European Court of Justice eventually made it clear that this exclusion was contrary to the European Directive the regulations were required to support. The UK government consequently deleted the exclusion clause, in 1993, and Tupe now clearly applies to public-sector transfers, even though there is often uncertainty about its application in individual cases.

Ambiguities about the precise definitions of undertakings and transfers mean that any disputed case has to be assessed on its particular facts. In general, however, it is reasonably clear that Tupe regulations must be adhered to in the majority of transactions when one business, or a discrete part of a business which retains its economic identity, is transferred to, sold to or merged with another business ('business' being defined broadly to include private- and public-sector organisations). In some doubtful cases the transferor and transferee agree to avoid differences of view by acting as though Tupe applies, even if a court might have decided otherwise.

The most important factors to be taken into consideration when managing a Tupe transfer operation, whether as a transferor or a transferee, are:

- identifying the employees concerned
- the protection of employees' contractual rights
- trade union recognition and collective agreements
- a definition of fair and unfair dismissals
- consultation with trade unions and elected employee representatives.

Meeting all the Tupe requirements and maintaining a high standard of employment practice involves both parties to the transfer. For the employees a transfer from one employer to another may well generate a great deal of stress and uncertainty. Morale and commitment may fall in the originating organisation in the period before the transfer takes place. The new employer may inherit a suspicious and resentful workforce. For both employers there is a risk that valuable staff may leave the organisation. To ensure as smooth a transfer as possible it is helpful for the two organisations to form a joint management project team to plan and oversee the whole transaction. This is often done to deal with the commercial and financial aspects of a transfer and to enable a potential new employer to assess the employment costs of the transferred staff. It is just as important for everything possible to be done to maintain staff morale during a period of inevitable uncertainty.

Identifying the employees

When the whole of a business is affected there is little difficulty in identifying which employees have Tupe transfer rights. It is important to note, however, that the regulations define employees quite widely, so that temporary workers who are in employment at the time of the transfer must be included, as must all part-timers. Those working under contracts for services (ie as self-employed or agency staff) are not covered. It is also important to relate the listing of the employees concerned to the date of the transfer, because the regulations apply only to those in employment immediately before the transfer occurs.

Matters may be less straightforward when only part of a business is transferred. Employees working for the whole of their time in the particular function are covered by Tupe, but others may work partly in the transferred function and partly elsewhere. For example, where a local authority is contracting out its grounds maintenance function there may be general-purpose employees who spend part of their time on this work and part on other, non-transferred duties. At what level of involvement in the transferred function do they acquire Tupe rights? The regulations are not clear on this point, but case law indicates that to be covered by Tupe employees must spend the bulk of their time on work in the transferred function – to the extent of at least 80 per cent and probably more. However, there is no reason for Tupe-style protection not to be afforded voluntarily to employees who may not meet a strict, legal interpretation of the regulations. This is one of the matters a joint management project team can consider.

Protection of contractual rights

Employees covered by Tupe are accorded two fundamental forms of protection:

- They retain full continuity of employment. They start work with the new employer as though there had been no break of service.
- They also retain their contractual entitlements relating to pay and conditions, with the exception of pensions. The new employer therefore has to take on the transferred employees on their current terms.

The pension position has caused some confusion. The regulations appear expressly to exclude from protection any rights accruing from an occupational pension scheme. Yet the government originally advised that in a Tupe transfer in the public sector a contractor should offer pension benefits which are 'broadly comparable' to those applying to the employees who are to be transferred. Regardless of any legal confusion, good employment practice suggests that the two parties to a transfer would be well advised to discuss the pension situation and, if possible, agree a solution which satisfactorily resolves the inevitable concern many employees will have about the effect of the transfer on their long-term pension entitlements.

The fact that employees transfer on their current terms does not mean that the new employer has to maintain these terms indefinitely. Once the direct link between the transfer and any alteration to terms has been broken, the normal principles of changes to contractual rights apply. There is as yet insufficient case law to indicate how much time must elapse after a transfer before this is taken to occur, though there are indications that the courts will not look kindly on any early change which has not been willingly agreed with all the employees concerned.

Trade union recognition

Tupe requires the new employer to take over any collective agreements applying to the transferred employees, presumably including relevant trade union recognition rights. To the extent that any such agreements are incorporated in individual contracts of employment, this causes no more problems than the protection of any other contractual rights. It may, though, cause industrial relations problems and is therefore best resolved by discussion – including negotiation with the relevant trade unions – before the transfer is made. In the public sector this has already led some major contractors in the waste disposal industry to sign new recognition agreements with trade unions which have a large public-sector membership.

Fair and unfair dismissals

Any dismissal (whether or not on grounds of redundancy) made by the current or the new employer, and which is effected to facilitate the transfer, is automatically unfair, the resultant penalties falling on the transferee. Any pressure on the current employer from the new employer to make the dismissal of certain employees a condition of the transfer should therefore be resisted. There is a provision, however, for fair dismissals to be made if economic, technical or organisational reasons entail changes in the workforce. Unfortunately, the regulations fail to define these words and their interpretation is consequently a matter of case law. In broad terms the new employer is able to restructure and reduce the size of the transferred workforce if this can be shown to be necessary for the efficient conduct of the business. But workforce reductions made primarily to ensure that the transfer goes ahead are not permitted.

Consultation

Consultation is a key element of the transfer process for both legal and good practice purposes. The legal requirement is for consultation to take place with recognised trade unions or elected employee representatives for the employees who may be affected by proposed transfer. Two particular points to note are:

- 'Affected employees' are not simply those who stand to be transferred. The transfer may well result in changes which affect other employees, such as alterations to work systems or changes in job location.

■ These other employees may be in either or both organisations, so both employers are likely to incur a legal duty to undertake consultations.

This joint responsibility is another reason for planned, co-ordinated action involving both managements. Consistent explanations of the reasons for the transfer need to be given to both workforces. The two groups of employees are likely to establish their own contacts, either informally or through their trade unions, and it is essential that the same accurate information is given to both. It is particularly helpful for the potential new management to meet the employees to be transferred in advance of the transfer in order to describe in detail what the transfer will involve and to highlight any advantages. Personal contact of this kind can convert a reluctant workforce into one which looks forward to the transfer. Visits to the new workplace, with introductions to future colleagues, can also contribute.

Tupe requires the subject matter of consultation to include:

■ when the transfer is expected to take place, and the reasons behind it
■ the 'legal, economic and social implications' of the transfer – although these terms are not defined
■ the 'measures' (again undefined) which the transferor and transferee plan to take in relation to the employees concerned.

Rather than attempting from case law to define the precise meaning of implications and measures it is better to explain everything about the transfer that employees want to know. Only commercially confidential information should be excluded. The aim is to ensure that the workforce is informed about every aspect of the transfer.

Further information

1 This chapter does not attempt to deal with every legal issue which can arise in a Tupe transfer. Expert legal advice should be sought for all but the most straightforward of transfers.

2 INCOMES DATA SERVICES. *Transfers of Undertakings.* Employment Law Handbook, Series 2, No. 2. London, 1995.

7   Teleworking

It has been predicted that teleworking will eventually become so popular that as much as one-third of all work could be performed outside the conventional workplace. These predictions have not yet come to pass, but there are indications that employers are becoming increasingly interested in the use of various forms of home-based working.

The primary benefit that employers gain from teleworking is generally seen as a reduction in office space costs. But employers also stand to gain from recruiting people who are unable to take up normal office employment, such as carers and disabled people; from access to alternative labour markets in different locations; and from the ability to retain staff who might otherwise leave because of personal circumstances or office relocation. Benefits for employees include personal control over flexible working time; and less time, energy and money spent on commuting to and from work.

Redesigning work and jobs
The decision to use teleworking should be based on an analysis and redesign of work and jobs, not just on the

grounds that computers have made it possible to move existing jobs out of the workplace. A technology-driven approach may miss some of the opportunities for teleworking which changes in work systems could offer, and operational problems can occur when the 'softer' work processes concerned with interpersonal contacts and peer support are overlooked.

Factors to consider include the pattern of work flow, the frequency and duration of different tasks, the extent of necessary checking or inspection, the amount of interaction between employees, and how easily outputs can be measured. Work processes that are ideal for teleworking tend to be individually driven, require minimal instructions and checking, need not be performed at set times, and produce measurable outputs.

Technical equipment

The standard equipment for most teleworkers is a PC, a modem, an answerphone and a fax, and these are often available in one integrated hardware package. It may be necessary to have an additional telephone line installed, and it is now possible to link the worker's own telephone into the company telephone network during working times. Some people also find it useful to have a small photocopier, a pager or a mobile phone.

The company should assess the cost of data transmission and advise the employee of the most cost-effective methods of communication. Telephone line charges should be met by the employer, as should the cost of insuring the equipment. But teleworkers would be well advised to check their own home building and contents insurance as well. Health and safety regulations apply to home-based employees, and this can affect furniture and the position of computer screens. It is not enough simply to issue employees with a package of equipment and leave it to them to site it and provide their own chair and a desk. Each home workplace should be inspected and passed as suitable and in line with health and safety standards.

Recruitment and induction

When teleworking is introduced within an existing workforce it is best to staff it with volunteers. Home-based work is not something to impose on unwilling or unsuitable employees and will, in any case, generally amount to a change in contractual conditions which should not be imposed unilaterally.

When employers recruit teleworkers from outside the company there are two important selection criteria to add to normal job competencies. First, ensure that the home environment is suitable – that the potential employee has satisfactory work conditions and will be able to give the necessary time and attention to the job. Second, check that candidates are temperamentally suited to working by themselves. A personality questionnaire may help to select those who have the necessary independence and self-motivation and who do not need constant social interaction.

Effective induction for teleworkers is even more important than for office-based staff. The latter learn a lot about the organisation from their informal contact with fellow employees, and are always immersed in the organisation's culture. Teleworkers need a more systematic process. Their induction programme should include office visits, introductions to the people they will deal with on the phone or via e-mail, and a full explanation of how their work fits into the organisation's activities overall.

Control and supervision

Conventional timekeeping and supervisory controls cannot be applied to teleworkers. Instead, the volume and quality of their work should be clearly specified and monitored. This is why work suitable for teleworking should have measurable outputs. How long a teleworker takes to complete a targeted outcome becomes irrelevant, provided the work is produced on time.

An important aspect of normal supervision is to help employees resolve difficulties and to correct faults. This is especially important for teleworkers, who may try to conceal flaws in their work and be reluctant to ask for help. A helpline could be set up to provide guidance, but supervisors should also visit teleworkers regularly to discuss any problems and check progress.

Communication and integration

An induction programme is only the start of what should be a continuous process of communication between the organisation and the teleworker – not simply to ensure that the work is done well but also to build rapport and develop a sense of belonging. Most organisations with teleworking experience say that the biggest non-technical problem with the system is the teleworker's feeling of isolation.

Measures to combat this, in addition to supervisory home visits, include a teleworkers' newsletter, to supplement normal staff journals; regular meetings of groups of teleworkers with their supervisors and their most frequent office contacts; inviting teleworkers to the organisation's social events; occasional study visits by groups of teleworkers to various parts of the organisation; allocating an office-based mentor to each teleworker, to whom the teleworker can talk informally and who can keep the teleworker up-to-date on office developments.

Training and development

Teleworkers have the same general training needs as other employees. They need help to raise their standards of competence and to keep up-to-date with new developments which affect their work. But unlike full-time office employees, teleworkers may be unable to attend conventional training courses, so it is the method of training, rather than its content, which needs special attention.

Fortunately, there has been a massive growth in the quantity of self-learning packages and distance-learning material available. This means that teleworkers with multimedia PCs can use CD-ROM and CD-i training material. The organisation itself may need to develop specific training packages for home-based learning. Where possible, this type of training should be linked to collective training events, even if these have to be arranged at unconventional times.

It should not be assumed that teleworkers are interested only in their current work – many have long-term career ambitions, sometimes including a wish in time to return to workplace jobs. Others might become teleworker supervisors, working from home with an office facility. To meet both immediate and long-term training and development needs, teleworkers should be included in appraisal systems, the appraisal interviews conducted at their homes.

Pay and benefits

Broadly speaking, teleworkers should be paid rates equivalent to those paid to office-based staff doing the same or comparable work. The principal and statutory requirement of equal pay for work of equal value still applies. The problem, however, may be that conventional pay relates to hours worked, which is rarely a satisfactory approach for teleworkers.

Some organisations require teleworkers to keep time-sheets showing a set total of weekly or monthly hours to qualify for a standard wage, but many teleworkers do not operate this way. They may work several short shifts on some days and none on others, interspersed with occasional long stints to complete specific tasks to a deadline. An uncheckable record showing a complicated pattern of irregular working times is not a sound basis for payment.

A far better way to reward teleworking is to pay for output – eg so many transactions or completed tasks per pay period – leaving it to the teleworker to decide how long to spend on this work. Rates can be based on an estimate of the time taken by a competent employee to achieve the targeted output, so the average pay level can be equivalent to either a full-time office wage or an agreed part-time proportion. Pay can be standardised within defined output limits so that minor variations in output do not change weekly or monthly wages. There may also be a need to guarantee a certain level of work (or pay) in order to avoid the uncertainty which can result from an over-simplified pay-by-results formula. There must be clear and fair rules about payment for additional work or increases in productivity.

Other conditions and benefits for teleworkers are best kept the same as for equivalent office-based employees. There is no reason, for example, why teleworkers should not be eligible for sick pay – and not just because they are less likely to be too sick for work than office-based staff. Unless teleworkers are treated as well as conventionally employed staff they will be perceived (and will perceive themselves) as second-class employees. If employers are to benefit from teleworking, it is important to give it at least the same status as equivalent, conventional forms of employment. This can be achieved only by giving teleworkers equal training, development, involvement, and pay and benefits.

Further reading

STANWORTH J. *and* STANWORTH C. *Telework: The human resource implications.* London, Institute of Personnel Management, 1991.

8   Managing redundancies

The increasing volatility of the competitive global market, together with pressure on costs, with business takeovers and mergers, and with the trend towards simpler organisation structures have all caused the management of redundancy to become a significant item on many personnel managers' agenda.

Managing redundancies effectively is not just a matter of compliance with the law. An organisation that handles a staffing surplus fairly and with sensitivity is also demonstrating a concern for its people which can contribute positively to its internal and public reputation.

Once the possible need for redundancy has been identified, the management of redundancies has four stages:

1   consulting with staff and trade unions
2   taking avoiding action
3   selecting staff for redundancy
4   providing assistance and compensation.

Some organisations already have well-defined procedures, often incorporated in collective agreements, covering all these stages. This chapter is intended primarily for organisations which have not codified their redundancy policies in this way.

Consultation

Some managers argue that to inform employees about possible redundancies at an early stage does little more than create a lengthy period of damaging uncertainty. Against this it must be recognised that sudden dismissals undermine staff confidence and can damage the organisation's public reputation. The difficulty of keeping possible redundancies secret should also be considered. The worst possible position is for management to lose control of the information process through leaks or rumours.

In any event, the timing and subject matter of collective consultation is not wholly a matter for the employer to decide. There are minimum statutory consultation periods, and although statute law does not require consultation with individual employees, case law – and good practice – does. Consultation with recognised trade unions or elected employee representatives must occur even if only one employee is involved, and whether or not the potentially redundant employees within the category covered by such recognition are union members, or are entitled to redundancy payments, or may volunteer for redundancy.

Informal consultation may begin at any time, but to meet the statutory requirements it is important to set out the following points in writing to the union within the legal time limits:

- the reasons for the proposed redundancies

- the estimated numbers (not names) and categories of employees involved
- the proposed method of selection for redundancy
- the proposed method and timing of dismissals
- the proposed method for calculating redundancy payments.

It is as well to obtain a receipt for this document. Two further requirements then arise: to consider any representations which may be made, and to reply, giving reasons for rejecting any of these representations. Consultation must also be conducted 'with a view to reaching agreement', implying genuine discussion of matters raised by the employees' representatives.

A failure to comply with these consultation requirements may result in the union or employee representatives' obtaining a protective award from an employment tribunal (formerly known as an industrial tribunal). This can require the employer to pay the employees concerned (whether still in employment or already dismissed) their full normal pay for such a period as the tribunal may decide, subject to maximum periods of 90 days (for 100 or more employees), 30 days (20 to 99 employees) or 28 days (fewer than 20 employees). The only escape from the consultation time limits is to establish that it was not reasonably practicable to adhere to them, although the courts tend to interpret this with some rigour. A failure to consult individual employees is almost always held by tribunals to be unfair. Consultation in this context means giving the employee an opportunity to ask questions, and perhaps suggest alternatives to redundancy, before the final redundancy dismissal is implemented.

Taking avoiding action

There is an expectation by the courts, staff and the public at large that employers should do all they can to minimise redundancies. The actions to consider include:

- phasing reductions to allow natural wastage to eliminate the staff surplus
- freezing external recruitment and giving potentially redundant employees priority in filling vacancies
- reducing or stopping overtime
- transferring work back in-house which is currently being undertaken by contractors, agency staff or consultants
- short-time working or temporary lay-offs
- exercising any contractual right to require the retirement of employees above normal retirement age.

Two other important avoidance measures are redeployment and retraining, assuming that the organisation has a need for additional or replacement staff in other jobs or locations. Some organisations give too little thought to the possibility of retraining across traditional job boundaries – from manual to non-manual work, for example. A careful assessment should be made of each employee's capabilities rather than making general assumptions about whole groups.

A key legal issue is whether or not the potentially redundant employees have a contractual obligation to transfer to other work or locations. If they have – and the requirement is unambiguous, supported by actual practice, and not wholly unreasonable – then such transfers can be effected outside the redundancy procedure. In most cases, however, transfers to other work (with or without retraining) or to other locations have to be by agreement. It is here that human resource planning pays off. Retraining can begin long before any formal action has to be taken about redundancy if business plans show a projected need for a change in skills requirement. A multi-skilled workforce is more able to adapt to changes in the proportion of different types of work and thereby avoid or reduce the incidence of redundancy.

The statutory provisions allow for redundancy entitlements to be set aside if an otherwise redundant employee unreasonably rejects the offer (and a four-week trial) of a suitable alternative job. There is a large body of case law on the subject of what constitutes suitability, and this can be decided only against the detailed circumstances of the person and job concerned.

Finally, there is the possibility of voluntary redundancies – a misnomer to the extent that to qualify for statutory redundancy payments an employee must be dismissed, not resign. In calling for volunteers, therefore, any documentation is best worded to show that employees are being asked to volunteer to be dismissed, not to resign. Many organisations have met their redundancy needs entirely on this voluntary basis, although this is influenced by the attractiveness of the compensation package.

Selecting employees for redundancy

If the avoidance measures do not resolve the situation, to decide on the criteria for selecting staff for redundancy becomes the next step. There are then three approaches. Firstly, if a collective agreement specifies the criteria, it must be adhered to. Departing from it (other than by a revised agreement) opens the door to legal action.

Secondly, in the absence of an agreement, custom and practice may have established recognised precedents. Last in, first out (LIFO) often applies on this basis. If these precedents are sufficiently strong, departing from them is almost as risky as breaking a formal agreement.

Thirdly, if neither of the previous conditions applies, then from a legal viewpoint the only two requirements are that the trade unions or employee representatives are consulted and that the criteria used are fair and reasonable.

There is an industrial myth that in the absence of any agreement or precedent LIFO must be used. That is incorrect. Among the legally acceptable criteria apart from length of service are performance standards, knowledge and skill, general conduct (provided it is assessed objectively), attendance and timekeeping.

Compensation and assistance

The law sets minimum standards for lump-sum redundancy compensation, although these statutory entitlements apply only to employees with at least two years' continuous service. In calculating statutory payments, weekly pay is limited to a maximum sum which is revised annually – £220 in 1998 – and length of service to 20 years. Many employers have decided that these statutory payments are inadequate and apply more favourable terms. Common differences from the statutory scheme are

- reducing the service entitlement from two years to one

- calculating entitlements on actual pay – ie not applying the statutory scheme's limit
- using the statutory scheme as a base but making specified additions, such as doubling the statutory payment
- using a different link between service and redundancy pay, such as a straight two or three weeks' pay per year of service, sometimes with an upper limit of one or two years' salary.

Other conditions of service may require particular attention:

- *pensions* – Depending on the employee's age, it may be decided to award additional pension entitlements and/or payment of an immediate early pension.
- *company cars* – The sudden withdrawal of a car may cause considerable problems for the employee. Some redundancy schemes allow an employee to continue to use a car for a period or to buy the vehicle on very favourable terms.
- *private medical insurance* – Membership of the organisation's group insurance scheme may be extended for a period beyond the date of redundancy.
- *loans* – Companies which operate various loan schemes may defer repayment of outstanding sums for a period.

To provide adequate support to redundant staff, more is needed than financial assistance, however generous. Redundancy is a traumatic event, and many employees need counselling and practical advice. In the case of large-scale redundancies it may be possible to open a job shop on the premises and for general advice to be provided through group information and discussion sessions. Assistance can be sought from local Job Centres or bought in from consultants or recruitment agencies.

In the case of small-scale redundancies employees can be counselled individually. For redundant managers many organisations now use outplacement consultants to provide training in job search activities, such as writing CVs and being interviewed, and assist the redundant manager to identify and contact possible new employers. The growth in the use of outplacement in recent years has been due in part to the difficulty busy personnel managers have in finding time to conduct intensive counselling. In addition, there has been a growing recognition that giving assistance is good employment practice.

Further information

1 INSTITUTE OF PERSONNEL AND DEVELOPMENT. *The IPD Guide on Redundancy.* London, Institute of Personnel and Development, 1996.

2 INCOMES DATA SERVICES. *Redundancy.* Employment Law Handbook, Series 2, No. 10. London, 1996.

3 ACAS. *Redundancy Arrangements.* Occasional Paper No. 37. London.

4 FOWLER A. *Redundancy.* London, Institute of Personnel and Development, 1993.

5 SUTER E. *The Employment Law Checklist.* 6th edn. London, Institute of Personnel and Development, 1997.

6 LEWIS D. *Essentials of Employment Law.* 5th edn. London, Institute of Personnel and Development, 1997.

Providing personnel capability

9   Structuring a personnel department

The management of organisational change has long been a major issue for the personnel function. Two related trends have dominated the redesign of organisation structures over the past decade: devolution and de-layering. Pushing decision-making out from the centre into operational units and flattening the management hierarchy continue to be features of organisational change in many companies and public services.

Although personnel managers' involvement in the redesign of business structures has sometimes been very limited, the personnel function has nevertheless been required to respond in two ways: by handling the many human resource issues involved in implementing organisational change, such as redeployment and redundancy, and by restructuring the personnel department itself to fit the new shape of the organisation. This reshaping of personnel departments is being influenced by another trend in management thinking: the devolution of operational personnel work to line managers.

There are difficulties in generalising about this subject.

The best structure for one organisation is not necessarily right for another, even when both have similar functions. Corporate culture and the organisation's mission and values need to be taken into account. What is devolved and which layers of management might be removed depend, among other things, on what the organisation considers important to retain at the centre. In the personnel field, for example, some multi-plant companies have localised their pay systems, while others consider it essential to retain a degree of centrally-driven company-wide pay consistency, although both may have devolved recruitment.

Faced with a need to review its own structure, a personnel department cannot, therefore, look for a general model. It must analyse its role, relative to the needs, shape and style of the business, and evolve a solution which ensures its organisational integration. The worst possible structure for a personnel department is one which sets it apart from the rest of the organisation.

Although this chapter cannot provide a blueprint for an ideal structure, it can provide a checklist of the issues to consider, and possible organisational responses.

Who does what?

The starting-point is to define which aspects of personnel work are to be handled by line managers and which by the personnel function. In recruitment and selection, for example, is the personnel function to decide on recruitment media and conduct interviews with all applicants? Or should line managers have the authority to do that, using the personnel function simply to process the administrative aspects of job advertising and advise on selection techniques?

The general trend is towards more line management involvement, but there are two very different approaches to that. One reduces the personnel function to largely administrative support. The other, while devolving much operational decision-making to managers (eg for selection), requires managers to meet defined standards of personnel practice. In other words, managers are given the authority to make many decisions about the management of their own staff provided they do so well. In this case, and using the example of selection, the personnel function does not get involved in interviewing but instead defines the quality standards for effective selection, arranges any necessary management training, and monitors how well managers handle the selection process.

Three possible types of role for the personnel function are, therefore,

- to undertake a wide range of detailed day-to-day operational personnel work on behalf of line managers (a role which has been common in the past but which has diminished in recent years)
- to provide largely administrative support to managers who handle their own operational personnel work
- to set quality standards for line managers' operational personnel activities, to provide support to managers to help them meet these standards, and to monitor the results.

Combinations of these variants are possible, involving different approaches for different personnel activities, and in all cases it is to be hoped that the organisation as a whole will wish to have a personnel input to top-level policy-making.

But differences of emphasis will have an effect on the function's staffing, structure and organisational location. So the stronger the emphasis is on standard-setting and monitoring, the more likely it is that the head of the function will be a member of the top management team. A bias towards non-strategic support to line managers may require a larger staff than the purely strategic function, but they are likely to be located lower down the hierarchy.

Three options

Assuming that the organisation is large enough to consider the employment by operational divisions of their own personnel specialists, three main options can be considered as alternatives to the conventional central department.

Firstly, it could retain personnel specialists at the centre but allow operational divisions to negotiate the range and cost of personnel services they obtain from the centre through service-level agreements. This is an option which has been widely adopted by local authorities. Its drawbacks include a risk of bureaucratic internal charging mechanisms and a restriction of personnel activities to those which can be pre-specified. It does not encourage personnel initiatives.

Secondly, it could keep personnel specialists executively responsible to the central personnel manager but outpost them to work within operational divisions. This establishes close working contact with line management and may be favoured by the personnel staff because they retain their professional identity. It falls short, however, of establishing a genuine multi-disciplinary team at divisional level, for line managers may see the outposted personnel specialists as central auditors.

Finally, it could maintain only a small central department dealing solely with strategic (or organisation-wide) issues, so that operational divisions employed their own personnel specialists. This is probably the most common private sector approach and is favoured by the Audit Commission for local authorities.

Although the last of these options has been the principal trend of the past decade, some organisations have found that it can lead to two problems. Firstly, the devolved personnel specialists can become so closely identified with their divisions – whose managers are probably pressing for ever-increasing autonomy – that they come to view the central personnel function as an influence to be kept at bay. To prevent this, the centre needs to specify the qualitative standards of human resource management it expects in its divisions, and divisional personnel specialists then have a responsibility to help their managements meet these standards.

Secondly, when moving from a centralised to a devolved structure, central staff who are being transferred out often fear professional isolation. This can be met by introducing the concept of 'head of profession' for the central personnel manager. He or she does not direct the work of divisional personnel staff but does retain a functional responsibility for their professional and career development. Regular meetings can be held of all the organisation's personnel specialists, who also have periodic individual career development discussions with the personnel head. It is also advisable to adopt a corporate policy which enables personnel staff to be transferred from division to division (and in and out of the centre) to ensure the necessary breadth of experience for them.

Generalist or specialist?

As soon as an organisation grows to a size at which more than one personnel professional is needed, choices have to be made between generalist or specialist appointments. Four options can be considered:

1 It could take a fully generalist approach, particularly if the centre is providing operational personnel services to divisions. Here each division has one nominated central contact for all purposes: its friendly in-house consultant. It is an approach less suited to a central strategic function, where a high level of expertise may be required in specific subject areas. The generalists in that case are the devolved divisional personnel staff.

2 The organisation could take a fully specialist approach, its top personnel team (under a generalist personnel manager) consisting entirely of remuneration, training and other specialists. This may suit the strategic centre if there is sufficient policy development and monitoring to warrant a specialist for each main subject. It is less satisfactory for the central function which is providing general personnel services to divisions. Divisional managers then have to decide which central specialist to approach, and may not make the right choice. For example, what a manager may

perceive as an IR problem may in reality require a training solution.

3   It is possible to have a mixed structure, so that generalists act as the first points of contact for their managerial customers and some specialists are available who the generalists can draw in to deal with particular issues. A possible problem here may be a reluctance among the generalists to seek specialist assistance.

4   There is another variant in which each central professional provides general personnel services to part of the organisation but additionally acts as a specialist across the organisation for one particular subject. Each is then the organisation's expert on this topic, for which he or she is able to provide high-level specialist assistance to colleagues in their generalist roles. This approach may suit organisations too small to justify separate teams of generalists and specialists but who still wish to tap a high level of specialist expertise. It requires a highly collaborative style of team working.

The most common specialist function is training, and a further variant on the four approaches just outlined is for this to be the only specialist role, sometimes on a largely free-standing basis, charging internal fees for course attendances. It is a common system for organisations which operate large in-house training programmes, possibly with a residential centre. However, with this approach there is a danger that training will become detached and not sufficiently responsive to the strategic and operational needs of the organisation.

Finally, the department must decide how its own

support staffing should be structured. Should each member of the personnel team have his or her own administrative support? Organisations with networked computers, a common personnel database and internal e-mail generally find a pooled information and administrative service satisfactory and cost-effective. A central information point, with a library of publications, training videos and the like, open to line managers as well as personnel staff, can also enhance the value and reputation of the personnel function.

For solo personnel managers in small organisations, all these options will appear as luxuries. They have to switch throughout the day between generalist and specialist roles, and between the strategic and operational. For them, obtaining specialist support is not a matter of internal organisation – it lies in tapping an external source, such as the IPD's information service, on an as-and-when basis, and using specialist external suppliers for functions or projects for which time or specialist know-how cannot be provided internally.

Further information

1 HACKETT P. *Personnel: The department at work*. London, Institute of Personnel Management, 1991.

2 FORSAITH J. *and* TOWNSEND P. *The Personnel Administration Handbook*. London, Institute of Personnel and Development, 1997.

3 FONDA N. *and* BUCKTON K. *Reviewing the Personnel Function*. London, Institute of Personnel and Development, 1995.

10 Outsourcing personnel services

Outsourcing – in the sense of buying in services from a supplier instead of managing them in-house – has long been a common practice for various aspects of people management. Some types of outsourcing are already well established through the use of agencies and consultancies for

- recruitment advertising
- recruitment and selection services, including testing and assessment
- training of all kinds – technical, professional and managerial
- outplacement and relocation services
- employee catering
- car leasing and fleet management.

Consultancies are also used extensively for time-limited projects such as organisational reviews, the design of reward systems, and employee attitude surveys.

What is new is partly the term 'outsourcing' itself, but more importantly, a significant growth in both the range of services on offer by specialist personnel and development suppliers and the extent to which organisations are using them. There is even debate over whether the whole personnel service might be an outsourced function. The *Personnel Manager's Yearbook* lists over 7,000 suppliers which, in addition to the services quoted above, can offer

- employee counselling and assistance
- occupational health services
- health and safety consultancy
- childcare services
- employee communication systems and programmes
- employment law advice
- equal opportunity audits and advice
- payroll management.

Part of the reason for the increase in outsourcing across many functions – not just in personnel – has been the core and periphery concept. The organisation focuses on its central or core role and buys in support services from external suppliers. Outsourcing has also been boosted by the government's programme of compulsory competitive tendering (CCT) of local government services and market testing in the Civil Service. Although the current government is pledged to phase out CCT, the principles of its replacement (best value) include a requirement to demonstrate cost-effectiveness. This implies comparing the cost and quality of in-house functions against external sources and using whichever delivers the best service. Outsourcing on a wide scale seems here to stay, although on a less prescriptive basis in the public sector than CCT.

The two principal approaches to outsourcing are market testing and formal tendering. Market testing may simply involve comparing the cost and quality of an in-house function against whatever information can be found about potential external providers. Even if an external provider is identified which is more cost-effective, the function is not necessarily outsourced. Instead, the organisation may decide to take action to raise the standard of the in-house function while keeping outsourcing as an alternative if improvements are not achieved. If a decision is taken to outsource, it may be effected through direct discussion with a selected supplier without making use of a formal tendering process.

In the case of formal tendering, the client organisation prepares a specification setting out the full requirements for the service and then invites tenders from interested potential suppliers. Selecting the successful bidder may then involve interviewing the short-listed suppliers and vetting their suitability through a process which has some similarities to the selection of candidates for jobs. Two approaches which aid this selection process are

- defining the required outcomes in the contract specification, and asking tenderers to indicate the methods and resources they would use to achieve these results: a specification for management training might thus stipulate an outcome of all trainees' obtaining NVQ Level 4 qualifications within a set time period, but ask how the training providers bidding for the contract would structure the training, and what training materials they would use
- interviewing the staff of the tenderers who would work on the contract. Tenderers may sometimes

make impressive formal presentations, led by their senior managers or consultancy partners, and then use other less experienced staff to run the contract. It is essential to meet the staff who will be directly involved – partly to be confident about their professional competence, but also to ensure compatibility of style and personality.

In considering the possible use of outsourcing for personnel and development functions, it may be useful to begin with considering the most extreme case: the possible buying-in of a complete personnel service. There are three main arguments against 100 per cent outsourcing. The first is that a significant proportion of personnel work is so central to the culture and strategic objectives of the organisation that it can be undertaken effectively only by the organisation itself. Because of this, personnel should be retained, at least in part, as an integral element of the business. The second point is more practical: the occurrence of situations such as industrial disputes which are often largely unpredictable but require immediate action when they arise. It is all but impossible to specify such tasks precisely enough to contract them out, or to find an external provider who can guarantee the instant and informed response they require.

This links to the third aspect, which is that there is, as yet, no significant market for the provision of a total personnel service. The exception may be a company that is too small to justify or afford its own personnel specialist and so pays an external consultant an annual retainer to advise on personnel issues, topped up by additional fees if an agreed total of consultancy days is exceeded. But in general the market for personnel services is characterised by hundreds of providers of different specialist services rather than by large organisations providing a complete personnel function.

Assuming, therefore, that outsourcing will usually apply only to some elements of personnel, the next stage is to decide which ones they should be. The first essential step is to identify the functions that will not be considered for outsourcing: activities that are integral to the core of the business, or where it is unlikely that an external provider could supply a sufficiently responsive service. Personnel departments whose staff all operate on a general basis with no functional specialisation may run into immediate difficulties. Any individual function subject to outsourcing must be able to be detached from other activities. Generalist personnel officers who handle recruitment, training, industrial relations and many other HR activities, and who move seamlessly between strategic advisory work and day-to-day personnel administration, may need to have elements of their work repackaged. Preparation for outsourcing may therefore involve reorganising the whole personnel function.

Identifying the elements to be retained at the core also highlights the importance of establishing at an early stage who will assume the role of client or purchaser. Who, for instance, will produce the specification for functions to be tendered? And who, if the end result is to use external providers, will oversee the contracts? Local government experience of CCT before it was extended to white-collar functions has demonstrated, sometimes painfully, that the quality of the effectiveness of an outsourced service can be at risk without a high level of expertise and influence on the part of the client. Producing specifications which clearly state the required outcomes, quality standards and timescales is particularly important. Managing an outsourced contract benefits from a collaborative or partnership relationship between client and supplier – although one in which the client is able to monitor the supplier's performance and retains the role of senior partner. Effective outsourcing should not result in any loss of overall control.

Once a function has been selected, the next stage is to check whether in its present form it is really what the organisation requires. There is no point, for example, in putting an outdated management training programme out to tender. Outsourcing provides an incentive to review the adequacy and relevance of many aspects of current personnel practice, and any decision about what parts of the function to outsource should be preceded by discussions with line managers about their real needs.

The criteria that eventually decide the outcome of an outsourcing exercise are cost and quality. It follows, therefore, that both factors need to be defined for the relevant in-house function before external comparisons can be made. Most HR departments know their total budgeted cost, but not all of them can break it down into functional components. This is essential for any true comparison. It may be necessary to introduce time-sheets to obtain data about the proportions of time (and money) spent by personnel staff on different activities, while expert financial assistance may well be required to ensure that overheads are being allocated correctly. Unit costs, such as the average cost per training day or per new recruit, and the hourly or daily costs of the personnel staff, often provide the best basis for comparisons with the external market.

Defining quality is more difficult. In the absence of quality criteria, decisions tend to be made solely on cost, although the cheapest service may well not be the best. Where relevant, comparisons can be made on such criteria as response times to information requests, success rates for vocational training, or the proportion of recruits who are assessed as fully satisfactory at the end of their probationary periods. Both market testing and formal tendering involve making judgements about the general quality of potential external providers. This assessment relies partly on assurances given by these providers about their ability to meet the quality standards defined in the service descriptions or contract specifications, but it is also necessary to decide which broader quality considerations should apply.

In 1995, the Institute of Personnel and Development (IPD), together with the Chartered Institute of Public Finance and Accountancy (CIPFA) and the Society of Chief Personnel Officers in Local Government (SOCPO), published a guide to the evaluation of quality in personnel CCT. This suggested that the overall quality of both potential contractors and the in-house function could be assessed on a points system. It involves scoring each organisation against a number of factors, such as

- know-how and experience
- access to specialist data and advice
- acceptability and relevance of proposed methods

compatibility of style or culture with that of the client organisation

price.

The factors could be weighted to reflect their varying importance between different outsourcing aims or projects – compatibility of style between the supplier and the client often being of all but overriding importance. The legal and administrative details of the tendering and market-testing processes are outside the scope of this chapter, but an honest, in-depth review of the in-house personnel function against these kinds of criteria would be useful preparation. As well as contributing to the selection of a suitable supplier, such a review might also lead to improvements that reduce the pressure for outsourcing, or strengthen an in-house bid when an existing function is put into competition with external suppliers.

Further information

1 *Compulsory Competitive Tendering for Personnel Services: The evaluation of quality.* London, Institute of Personnel and Development/Chartered Institute of Public Finance and Accountancy/Society of Chief Personnel Officers in Local Government, 1995.

2 AP Information Services. *Personnel Manager's Yearbook.* Updated annually.

3 White R. *and* James B. *The Outsourcing Manual.* Aldershot, Gower, 1996.

11 Benchmarking the personnel function

A benchmark, in its original meaning, is a short groove cut into the stone cornice of a building and marked by an arrow, the height of which above sea level has been accurately measured. Surveyors use it as a reference point when measuring the heights of other locations in the vicinity. Benchmarking within organisations is similar in principle. In essence, a company measures its performance against that of other companies to assess whether its standards are higher or lower.

But there is far more to benchmarking than making statistical comparisons. Such a simple approach may amount to no more than what one expert in the field has described as 'industrial tourism' – collecting snapshots of what others are doing, but failing to examine the reasons for differences in performance, and not using the data to identify and develop best practice. The key to using benchmarking effectively is to undertake it only if the aim is to achieve improvements. There is little point in spending time and effort collecting comparative data for its own sake, or if its use by managers is only to justify current standards. This may seem obvious but self-justification is a common management reaction to benchmark data. For instance, if a firm has an above-average ratio of personnel staff per 100 employees, the managerial response may be 'That's because we set higher standards.' But if the ratio is below average, the reply might be 'We are more efficient.' In the absence of further study, neither statement can be taken as correct, and if benchmarking goes no further than data collection, it has been a waste of time.

There are four main stages to effective benchmarking:

- selecting aspects of performance that can be improved, and defining them in a way that enables relevant comparative data to be obtained – in effect, producing performance indicators that will make sense to other organisations
- choosing relevant organisations from which to obtain raw or headline data
- studying this data to identify possible opportunities for improvement and then examining the procedures of the best-performing organisations to pick up ideas that can be adopted or adapted to achieve performance improvements
- implementing any new processes.

Comparative performance indicators

In selecting performance indicators that will form the basis of initial data collection it is helpful to distinguish between input and output measures and, when practicable, to place priority on the latter. It is often easier to define inputs than outputs. Examples of input measures include staffing ratios, per capita expenditure on training or, in manufacturing companies, the varying proportions of labour, materials and overhead costs.

The drawback with many measures, whether of inputs or outputs, is that they rarely provide an indication of quality. Take, for example, the widely used indicator of response time to customer inquiries. This provides only part of the picture because it gives no indication of the quality of the service. Apparently good figures may conceal significant customer dissatisfaction, while longer response times may coincide with the clients' being delighted with the results.

Ideally, best practice involves high standards in both inputs and outputs. Indices of customer satisfaction are one form of output measurement. Some personnel departments conduct surveys in which their internal clients – the line managers – are asked to rate the quality of the various services provided by the department. If other organisations conducting similar surveys can be found, these ratings can form part of a benchmarking study and may indicate areas where a change of procedure could lead to improvements.

Selecting relevant comparators

There are two different approaches – general and selective – to choosing organisations from which to obtain comparative data. The main purpose of the former method is to produce a wide range of performance measures across an entire sector. Examples of general data sources include the government's ratings of pupil performance in every primary school, the Audit Commission's performance indicators for local authorities, and APAC, the personnel database developed by the MCG consulting group.

Headline data of this kind is useful, but it must be considered with caution. Misleading conclusions can be drawn from individual performance indicators when they are viewed in isolation. For instance, a major weakness of the schools' performance data is that no information is provided about factors that have a significant impact on test results. A comparison of a school's position in the league tables and the result of its Ofsted assessment often shows little correlation between the standards implied by test results and wider assessments of the quality of its education.

Correlating information can add considerable value to headline data. In the HR field, for example, comparative data about employee absence rates is more likely to be relevant if set against information about the type of work and the size and constitution of the workforce. General data may be obtained through participation in studies by professional institutions or commercial organisations. National salary surveys by specialist consultancies are an established source of pay benchmarks. They are particularly useful when categorised by industrial sector, company size and job type, and supplemented by data about non-pay benefits. It is also worth while finding out whether other similar organisations run benchmarking clubs, and if they do not, to consider starting such a club.

A more selective approach is required when an aspect of performance that requires attention has already been identified. This may be triggered by an initial study of general comparative data that suggest other firms are performing better, or by internal concerns generated by poor results, operational problems or customer complaints. In this case it is necessary to identify organisations of a broadly similar nature – preferably those with a reputation for effectiveness in the relevant activity.

Although much of the initial data may be obtained through a well-designed questionnaire, it is often helpful to make personal contact first to explain the process, explore the best ways of describing the type of information sought, guarantee confidentiality, and offer to circulate an anonymous summary of the results to all participants. With topic-based benchmarking it is possible to collect more data about a single issue than can be obtained from a general survey. It may also be feasible to ask participants to supplement their answers by sending details of specific policies, such as copies of absence control procedures or performance appraisal guidelines.

There are two types of benchmark data that may be difficult to obtain: commercially sensitive information and reliably comparative cost data. Commercial sensitivity, as evidenced by a reluctance to exchange details of unit costs or profit margins, must be respected. The cost of activities or systems that are not sensitive is essential when assessing cost-effectiveness, but the results can be seriously misleading unless the same costing conventions are used in all organisations. An aspect that often causes problems in ensuring like-for-like financial data is the method used to calculate overheads on the direct costs of functions such as training and recruitment. In this case it may be wise to seek specialist accountancy advice when devising a questionnaire and interpreting the data.

Identifying potential improvements

The purpose of obtaining benchmark data needs to be kept firmly in mind: to identify potential improvements in performance. Once such opportunities have been spotted, the more intensive aspects of benchmarking can begin. These go beyond the study of comparative statistics and the documentation of other people's procedures. They involve a detailed on-the-ground study of the methods of high-performing organisations. Understandably, this requires the full co-operation of those concerned, although it is encouraging that many companies are willing to provide extensive information and facilities.

The organisations that have benefited from this aspect of benchmarking recommend the use of study teams which include staff from different functions and levels. For instance, a benchmarking team aiming to raise standards in BP's personnel function consisted of a mix of line managers and personnel specialists. And when the Belfast-based aircraft manufacturer Short Brothers visited companies throughout the UK to study examples of good personnel practice, it included secretaries and support staff in its touring teams.

Implementation

The final stage of the benchmarking process is the implementation of new systems. Here it is important to recognise that the success of other businesses may be influenced by the motivational and cultural context in which their systems operate as much as by the technical characteristics of the systems themselves. As a result, one of the issues for study teams to investigate is the nature of the whole work environment – physical and psychological – in which best practice flourishes.

Further information

1 BURN D. *Benchmarking the Human Resource Function.* London, Technical Communications, 1996.
2 BRAMHAM J. *Benchmarking for People Managers.* London, Institute of Personnel and Development, 1997.

12 Introducing quality into personnel

Fiercely competitive market conditions and the drive to cut costs have led organisations to question whether support functions such as personnel are adding value or are dispensable overheads. But attempts to measure the contribution of a personnel unit solely in financial terms have proved difficult. Low unit training costs, for example, give no indication of the relevance or effectiveness of training, while the personnel manager's advice on matters such as organisational culture is even more difficult to assess in statistical terms.

An emphasis on cost reductions has consequently been paralleled in many cases by a concern for quality. This trend has had potential benefits for personnel, both in the contribution it can make to achieving quality goals across the organisation as a whole, and in the application of quality principles to the way the function itself operates. Moreover, because any effective assessment of the value of a personnel unit must to a large extent be qualitative, a focus on quality provides a more realistic approach to this assessment than previous attempts to produce financial cost-benefit analyses.

While noting the support the function can give to quality programmes generally (and particularly in training and employee communications), this chapter addresses the application of quality management principles to the personnel function itself. Four aspects to consider are:

- the assessment of the function's current quality
- quality assurance (QA) and ISO 9000 approaches
- the total quality management (TQM) approach
- the qualitative characteristics of the effective personnel unit.

Assessing current quality

Quality is not an absolute concept. Within any organisation the quality of the personnel function is a matter of its relevance to the style, values and aims of the organisation as a whole. Before embarking on a quality programme it is therefore necessary to establish the function's current quality standards and decide whether changes are needed. The quality programme can then be focused on those personnel activities which most affect the function's contribution to organisational success.

Some statistical indicators may be useful at this point, particularly if it is possible to get comparative data from other, similar organisations. Examples include the ratio of personnel unit staff to total employees, the ratio of professional personnel staff to their office support staff, employee turnover and absence rates and trends, and per capita recruitment and training costs. While comparisons need to be treated with caution, and while high or low figures relative to other organisations are not proof of high or low quality, significant variances may at least indicate aspects worth detailed investigation.

The more significant elements of the assessment are the views of the function's managerial 'customers', of which some personnel units now undertake periodic and systematic surveys. One approach is to ask senior line managers to list their key operational objectives. These objectives are then set against a schedule of the main services provided by the personnel unit – recruitment, training, industrial relations advice, etc. For each operational objective, and for each personnel service, the managers are then asked to state whether the personnel unit's activities have aided, impeded or had no impact on the achievement of the particular objective. Where neutral or adverse results occur, managers are then interviewed to discover the reasons.

There are other ways in which managers' views can be obtained, but the important principle is that only by asking them can the personnel function discover whether, in the view of management, a quality service is being provided. Whatever the precise form of this kind of survey, two points are worth noting. Firstly, if the survey is conducted periodically, the same approach should be followed each time so that trends can be identified. Secondly, it is important to obtain the corporate view of the chief executive and the board (or top management team) as well as those of individual managers. The role of the personnel function is not solely to satisfy the heads of various line units. It is also to contribute to the achievement of corporate goals – a role which may sometimes require the stance taken by individual managers to be challenged.

Quality assurance and ISO 9000
A survey of managerial views may produce adverse comments about current personnel procedures considered

inadequate or too restrictive. Even in the absence of any specific managerial criticism it may be helpful to review and revise the function's current set of systems and processes.

Any concern about procedure points to the adoption of a quality assurance (QA) approach. The essence of QA, as applied to functions such as personnel, is the design and operation of systems and procedures which will ensure the consistent delivery of services of the necessary quality. Its introduction is usually linked to a redefinition of quality standards in the light of surveys of the organisation's needs. It is important to note that the procedural aspects of QA do not necessarily guarantee high quality – only consistent quality. To take an extreme example, one personnel unit may set a target of replying to all job applicants within five days; another may decide not to reply to unsuccessful applicants at all unless they specifically enquire why they have heard nothing. A QA approach can be adopted by both units to ensure their very different quality targets are met consistently, although the latter is hardly an example of good practice.

The international quality standard ISO 9000 (or BS 5750) is in the mainstream of the QA approach, and some personnel units have obtained this formal certification. Whether it is appropriate to spend the time and money needed to obtain this award is a matter for organisations to decide for themselves, but the principles of the standard can be followed, whether or not formal certification is sought. The main elements are:

 producing a written quality policy statement setting out what the whole system is designed to achieve
 reviewing how every aspect of the unit's activities

is performed, identifying inconsistencies, gaps in the definition of sound practice or inappropriate systems

- redesigning or introducing all necessary processes and producing a comprehensive procedure manual which codifies good practice and specifies the targeted quality standards
- ensuring that procedures include the keeping of adequate records which contain the information needed to assess whether quality standards are being maintained
- training staff in the revised or additional procedures
- introducing some form of periodic monitoring of the effectiveness of the procedures.

There is a potential danger with QA if it is seen as being concerned primarily with securing rigid adherence to procedures. As an early report of the Personnel Standards Lead Body indicated, a common criticism of personnel specialists by top managers is 'an over-concern with rules and procedures amounting sometimes to inappropriate policing and blocking action'. It needs to be recognised that the real purpose of QA is not to produce procedures *per se* but to secure the right quality of service. As a result it may be necessary to introduce a process for departing from standard procedures when this best serves the organisation's needs.

Total quality management

TQM is sometimes seen as an alternative or even opposite approach to QA, although in many cases it is better to consider the two as complementary. TQM is essentially concerned with the overall culture of the organisation and the attitudes and motivation of managers and employees at large. At its simplest it is a programme of leadership, exhortation and training to engender an enthusiasm throughout the workforce for achieving the highest possible quality standards and to search continually for improvement. In reality, enthusiasm without a framework of supportive systems (ie QA) will probably be as ineffective as a procedure manual operated without a real commitment to quality.

For the personnel function a TQM approach depends on the example set by the head of the unit. Only if he or she is seen by the unit's staff as deeply committed to doing the right things to the highest possible standard is it likely that the work of the unit as a whole will gain a reputation for high quality. The essential elements of the approach include continuous contact with the unit's internal customers to ensure their needs are fully understood; the involvement of all the unit's staff (not just the professionals) in periodic reviews of how well they are doing and whether there are things that could be improved; and, when things do go wrong, an attitude of 'What can we learn from this mistake?' rather than 'Who is to blame?'

The qualities of an effective personnel unit

Although the detailed features of effective personnel units vary depending on each organisation's specific needs, there are three qualities which are common to all.

Firstly, good personnel units are professionally knowledgeable. The personnel manager is recognised as the organisation's expert on all relevant aspects of people management, and on the constitution and the characteristics of the organisation's workforce.

Secondly, they are proactive. Personnel's advisory role is interpreted positively, and the function initiates proposals for action rather than just reacting to events or waiting to be asked for assistance or advice.

Finally, a good unit is relevant. Its initiatives, procedures and style are all perceived by line and corporate management as contributing to the organisation's immediate and long-term business objectives.

Further information

1 COLLARD R. *Total Quality: Success through people*. 2nd edn. London, Institute of Personnel Management, 1993.

2 FONDA N. *and* BUCKTON K. *Reviewing the Personnel Function*. London, Institute of Personnel and Development, 1995.

Getting your message across

13   Attitude surveys

It is important for any organisation to know the reputation it has among its employees. Is it, for example, considered a good or poor employer? Are its managers respected or mistrusted? Do people gain job satisfaction from their work? In addition to such general points, information on specific issues may be needed – for example, employees' views about a performance-related pay scheme or the extent to which they understand and support a customer care policy. Periodic surveys which repeat the same questions can also reveal trends and show whether action taken as a result of an initial survey has had its intended effect.

Preparation
It can be damaging to employee morale to launch an attitude survey without considering its immediate and long-term impact. The act of conducting a survey has an effect on employee attitudes, regardless of its content. It amounts to a message to employees that their views are considered important, so any subsequent failure either to explain or take action on the results is likely to generate cynicism or resentment. And if people are consulted once

in this way, they may understandably feel they should be consulted again later. It is consequently advisable to consider whether surveys should become a standard element in the organisation's personnel processes before embarking on one for the first time.

There are several issues to be addressed in the preparatory stage:

- *the survey's purpose* – Is it to determine attitudes across a broad spectrum (such as employees' perception of management style) or to monitor views on specific issues, such as the pay and benefits system?
- *the extent of management support* – Although the personnel department will probably be responsible for carrying it out, the survey needs to be seen by employees and managers alike as something the organisation considers important and necessary. Without clear support from the top, managers may perceive a survey as a threat – a way of enabling disgruntled employees to complain about them. One factor which contributes to the success of a survey is the ability and willingness of managers to explain its purpose to their staff and encourage full participation.
- *communication with employees* – It is important to explain fully why and how the survey is being held and to provide guarantees of confidentiality. Employees are often initially cautious about participating, and unless they are reassured that their individual views will not be relayed to their managers in an attributable form the survey may

well fail. The communication process also needs to cover the whole exercise, from launch to announcements about its results.

Design and piloting

Once the general scene has been set, the next stage is to determine precisely what form the survey should take. The first point to consider is whether or not to use consultants. An organisation which has no previous experience of surveys and no expertise in their design would be ill-advised to mount a survey without professional assistance. The involvement of an external organisation may also help to reassure employees on impartiality and confidentiality.

The next decision is on the survey's format. There are two main variants: questionnaires and interviews. Questionnaires are particularly useful where large numbers are involved and where the information can be obtained from tick- box answers. Interviews – which may be individual or structured group discussions – can provide greater insight into underlying attitudes and perceptions, but they are time-consuming and impracticable for large numbers.

A further decision then needs to be taken on whether the survey is to be held on a census basis (ie covering all employees) or directed at a targeted or random sample. The first of these is appropriate when an assessment of general attitudes is required across the whole workforce. A targeted group may be sufficient if the survey is focused on issues of primary concern to only part of the workforce (eg views about the pension scheme among employees over 50). Random selection, either for questionnaires or for interviews, can provide statistically sound data but may be resented by non-selected employees who would like to have been asked their views.

Questionnaires are the most commonly used method, but their design requires considerable expertise. They should be capable of fairly quick completion. Few people will spend more than 20 minutes working through a series of questions. Box-ticking should be used as much as possible, but with space for optional written comments. It is better to present an even number of potential answers for questions with several alternative responses: with an odd number, respondents tend to pick the middle answer. Consideration should also be given to what permutations or correlations of answers should be analysed, and to the need to be consistent about the categories used in different questions (eg all age ranges should be the same). It is also important to ensure that questions are unambiguous, that each refers to only one factor, and that they carry no implication of race or gender bias. If employee numbers are large and if many correlations are to be examined, the questionnaire should be designed for computer analysis.

Before launching a questionnaire it should be tested on a pilot group. Piloting will often reveal ambiguities or responses which the designer did not anticipate. Similarly, a trial interview will show whether the planned structure and content will encourage a free flow of employee responses. If individual interviews are to be used, it is essential to decide in advance what questions to ask, and in what order. A skilled interviewer may probe initial answers by open-ended follow-up questioning, but underlying consistency is essential if comparable information is to be obtained from all participants.

Implementation and analysis

How a questionnaire is issued, the time allowed for its completion, and how it is to be returned all have an influence on the response rate. Another factor to be considered is whether the questionnaires are to be distributed within the workplace. If the organisation has a system of briefing groups, it may be a satisfactory method in that managers can be provided with standard briefing data for answering employees' questions. Alternatively, questionnaires can be issued by the internal or external post. This may increase the administrative work and cost, but it will ensure that the same explanations about completion are given to all staff, and help convince them of the value the company places on their response.

Decisions are also needed on whether questionnaires are to be completed during working time or taken home. If they are completed at work, a higher response rate may be achieved, and answers will not be influenced by family or friends. Some staff may, however, prefer to give more thought to their answers than could be allowed for in a short working period.

Confidentiality

How are the completed questionnaires to be returned? This is of critical importance, particularly if any concern exists – despite assurances – about confidentiality. The worst possible method is for managers to collect open completed forms. A more satisfactory method is for questionnaires to be returned under sealed cover to the personnel department, although even this may not put all suspicion at rest if employees think they could be individually identified from the information they may have been asked to supply about such matters as job category, grade, gender and location.

Partly for reasons of confidentiality and partly because of the work involved in statistical analysis, external organisations are often used for the receipt and analysis of questionnaires. Staff are provided with postage-paid envelopes for the return of their forms to the organisation concerned, together with a statement from that organisation explaining their role and a guarantee of anonymity when producing the analysis and report. Examples of such organisations would be consultancies specialising in the design, administration and analysis of attitude surveys; more general HR and employee communications consultancies; specialist research organisations, often human resource units of firms involved in public opinion surveys and market research; relevant departments in colleges and universities; computer bureaux with a bias towards statistical analysis; and the Electoral Reform Society.

For a survey of any complexity, the way the results are reported needs to be carefully considered. Personnel managers need a full set of raw data to look for possible correlations, but for senior management key policy-level issues need to be identified. It is easy to swamp major issues with a mass of interesting but not crucial data, and the emphasis in management reporting needs to be on matters which call for significant action.

Action and monitoring

After a survey is completed, a report for management and employees should be issued immediately. The report must be totally honest, with no attempt to gloss over anything adverse to the organisation. It should also thank employees for their co-operation and give a commitment to corrective action.

Following an extensive general survey, a manager can be nominated to head a project team to develop action plans and assist in their implementation. Periodic progress reports to managers and employees will help to maintain interest and combat potential criticism that the messages revealed by the survey have not been listened to. Assuming that an action plan has been implemented, questions will then arise over its effectiveness. The best way of monitoring this is by running another survey asking many of the same questions, although this should not be done too soon after the initial survey. Attitudes and perceptions rarely change quickly, and there is also the risk of a very early re-survey picking up short-term reactions rather than measuring the lasting impact of the action plan.

Further information

WALTERS M. *Employee Attitude and Opinion Surveys*. 2nd edn. London, Institute of Personnel and Development, 1996.

14   Suggestion schemes

Suggestion schemes have been a traditional element in most organisations' personnel practices, although many schemes are all but moribund. A figure of one suggestion per year for every 10 employees has been quoted as the UK average, which would mean that some schemes exist in which the participation rate is even lower. These figures are in sharp contrast to those of a few highly successful schemes where the annual average is close to four suggestions from every employee.

Organisations that do not stimulate a flow of ideas from their employees are missing significant advantages which a successful suggestion scheme can provide. There is the obvious benefit of suggestions which reduce waste, improve productivity and cut costs. Improvements in quality will also enhance the organisation's reputation with its customers. Beyond these direct benefits, an effective suggestion scheme demonstrates to employees that they are valued as intelligent people with an interest in the success of their organisation. Good suggestion schemes can contribute to the creation of a committed workforce.

There are a number of options which organisations should consider when designing a suggestion scheme.

- Should it be a permanent scheme or run as a time-limited campaign?
- Should rewards be related solely to cost savings, or should wider criteria such as quality or customer service be used?
- Should suggestions be limited to individual employees, or should team suggestions also be encouraged?
- Should rewards be given only for suggestions which are adopted or should employees also be rewarded for the initiative involved in making suggestions, regardless of outcome?
- Should the reward be monetary or comprise an incentive of another form?
- Should the value of rewards be calculated by a fixed formula, or should a less rigid or more subjective approach be adopted?

There are also factors to consider about the scheme's administration – in particular, whether or not to use a committee and/or a scheme administrator. Before deciding some of these details it is important to note the Inland Revenue's criteria for tax-free awards. In summary, the following rules apply:

- The scheme must be formally constituted and open to all employees on equal terms.
- Awards must be for suggestions outside the scope of employees' normal duties.
- Tax-free 'encouragement awards' (for suggestions

which are not implemented) are subject to a maximum of £25.

▪ Tax-free awards for successful suggestions must not exceed 50 per cent of the anticipated net benefit in the first year, or 10 per cent of the expected net benefit over 10 years – in either case subject to an upper limit of £5,000.

Ideally, a scheme should be a standing element of the organisation's motivation strategy, stimulating a continuous flow of ideas across the whole workforce. To achieve this requires far more than the detailed design of the scheme itself. Employees will rarely respond on any significant scale unless the culture of the organisation – and particularly its management style – encourages employee participation.

When a scheme has become moribund, or when no scheme has previously been operated, interest may best be generated or regenerated by launching a highly-publicised and time-limited campaign. This may usefully be part of a wider programme of cultural change such that the interest and excitement of a high-profile short-duration scheme is symbolic of the organisation's new emphasis on recognising employee talent.

To be successful a campaign needs to have enthusi-astic and intensive management support, to be given a name (eg 'Bright Ideas'), to be widely and continuously publicised, and probably to offer non-cash prizes rather than finely calculated monetary awards. There is a strong case, too, for giving all participants some form of reward or prize, however small, except for obviously frivolous suggestions.

Traditional schemes place a sole or primary emphasis on suggestions which achieve cost savings. Although this objective may be the most important for the organisation, it restricts the range of good ideas and may also convey an unintended message to employees that all the organisation cares about is money. It is therefore worth while encouraging suggestions which improve quality and customer care, whether or not direct financial benefits can be calculated.

Traditionally, suggestion schemes have sought ideas only from individuals, but this conflicts with the growing emphasis in many organisations on teamworking. Where quality circles are operating, these small groups can be a major source of ideas not just on the work within their normal scope (which does not qualify for tax-free awards) but also on other topics relevant to the success of the business. Provision for team as well as individual suggestions and awards is desirable in most schemes.

Practitioners have different views on whether awards should be restricted to suggestions which are implemented, or should be given to reward the effort and interest involved in submitting them, regardless of their practicability. This is influenced in part by the culture of the organisation and by whether or not the scheme is permanent, as well as by the tax rules. There are certainly problems for a standing scheme if all suggestions are rewarded, although a restrictive approach to implementation will soon kill a scheme if this results in very few participants' receiving recognition. In a time-limited campaign there is a strong case for recognising every suggestion with a small, immediate award, and later, larger sums or prizes for suggestions which are eventually implemented.

It is important in the early stages of a scheme, or during a short-run campaign, to stimulate interest and give encouragement by rapid recognition. This may be by something as small as a specially designed tie or scarf, provided that such awards are seen as tokens of recognition rather than as expressions of the value of particular suggestions.

Schemes with cost savings as their sole or primary objective normally calculate awards in relation to the suggestions' financial value. Percentages of the first year's savings may range from 10 per cent to 50 per cent, or from 5 per cent to 10 per cent of the estimated savings over five years. However, this commonly-used approach may inhibit the submission of suggestions which would generate only very small savings. Staff may think the effort of making such suggestions not worth the very small awards which would result. Interestingly, though, Japanese companies achieve large numbers of suggestions without the lure of big rewards for the occasional major idea. The emphasis is on *kaizen* – continuous improvement by a multitude of small steps – and some UK firms are adopting this approach.

An alternative to financial rewards is the use of a potentially wide variety of non-cash awards. These are particularly effective in a time-limited suggestion campaign, when the best ideas submitted within the period of the campaign can be rewarded by prizes such as holiday vouchers, cameras, TVs, etc. This type of award can also figure in standing schemes, when competitions can be run between departments for the best or largest proportion of suggestions each month. Non-cash team awards, such as visits to a show or a day trip on

Concorde, can also be used both to reward team-based suggestions and reinforce team spirit.

Although published cost-benefit formulae provide employees with the guarantee of a certain level of reward, they may have disadvantages, particularly when they are subject to an arbitrary upper limit. Occasionally, an employee may produce an outstanding suggestion which will generate extremely large savings but for which the formula will produce a relatively small sum. This can result in adverse publicity both for the organisation and for suggestion schemes in general. It is also difficult to calculate awards when the suggestion has resulted in qualitative improvements. For these reasons an alternative approach may be used, such as a five-point scale with suggestions rated for their importance or ingenuity, with a set range of awards to match. Even within a formula-based scheme provision can be made for exceptional awards for the occasional exceptionally valuable idea – even though sums exceeding £5,000 will be taxed.

To be successful, a scheme needs efficient administration with emphasis on the immediate acknowledgement of all suggestions and as speedy a decision about their outcome as the necessary investigations will permit. Any large organisation which succeeds in generating suggestions at the rate of several a year per employee may require a full-time administrator who can also handle the often complex issue of patenting.

It is also important that managers give the scheme the priority it deserves, and if asked to assess a suggestion, do so promptly and constructively. Although committees are often used to make the final decision about implementation and awards, they are not necessarily the most effective form of vetting. A sufficiently senior administrator, guided by relevant technical and managerial assessments, may well be found to be a better approach. The cost of administration is soon recovered by the improvements achieved through a continuous flow of employees' ideas.

Part of the administrator's function is to ensure that the scheme is given adequate promotion and publicity. Standing schemes need refreshing from time to time by special events, awards ceremonies, competitions between units or teams, and occasional additional campaigns targeting specific themes such as energy savings or waste reduction. Running a successful scheme needs as much continued effort and imagination as any other important aspect of HR management – it cannot be left to run itself.

15 Keeping employees informed

Keeping employees well informed should be only part of a wider strategy to secure employee commitment. Other elements may include various forms of consultation, quality circles, and the way work itself is structured. But an organisation that is embarking on a programme of action to raise the level of employee interest and commitment may well find improvements in its information practices easiest to implement as a first stage. What must be kept in mind, however, is that employees who are better informed will almost certainly feel more strongly than before that they should be able to comment on and influence managerial decisions. Better information leads to more active forms of employee involvement.

An effective information strategy needs to address two main questions:

What information should employees be given?
What are the best means of providing this information?

Employees' information requirements can be examined

from the viewpoints of the individual employee and of the organisation. The two main objectives are to satisfy the employees' interest in, and curiosity about, the organisation and its activities, and to provide them with whatever additional information is necessary to ensure an intelligent understanding of the organisation's aims and circumstances.

The interests of individual employees start with matters specific to their own jobs and then expand outwards. The first requirement is to know the purpose of the employee's job and how it fits with the work of immediate colleagues. This leads on to an explanation of the role of the employee's unit or team. That in turn can be extended to show how the unit contributes to the activities of the whole function or department. The picture is completed by information about the organisation as a whole, including the role the organisation plays in its particular external economic or functional environment.

For each of these spheres of interest, there are three dimensions which need consideration:

1 *background or historical information* – Why was the job established, and who were the present employee's predecessors? How long has the section or division been in its present form? What is the organisation's history – has it been growing or shrinking? What have been the main crises or achievements of the past?

2 *an update of current issues* – How well is the job being done? How is the section or division regarded by the rest of the organisation? What are the current problems, achievements and opportunities at job, section, divisional and organisation levels?

3   *information about the future* – What plans or problems are there which might change the nature of the work, create job risks or opportunities, or lead to changes to the organisational structure?

In essence, the employees' needs are to understand the context in which their jobs are placed and to have an understanding of the nature of, and reasons for, likely changes. Running through this is an interest in personalities as well as events. They may need to know who founded the company, who the current directors and managers are, and something about them as people – not just their formal organisational roles.

In addition to meeting employees' information needs, there are at least three additional objectives for an information strategy. It can

- promote an understanding of, and commitment to, the organisation's mission and values
- break down attitudinal barriers between occupations or functions and generate a more integrated workforce
- ensure the workforce understands the economic realities affecting the organisation's activities.

The first of these points can be illustrated by an organisation which embarks on a new customer care programme. The message that the customer is king and that all employees should reflect this in everything they do is one which should permeate every aspect of the employees' information system. Messages about such matters as customer care, total quality or cost economies should address three questions: What do we need to do? Why is it important? and How should it be done?

The second objective is concerned with helping employees in each occupation or section to understand how all these apparently separate activities contribute to the well-being of the whole. Large organisations in particular are subject to a low level of collaboration between different sections when each considers itself to be more important than the others. Information which demonstrates the interdependence of parts can help to break down these barriers.

Thirdly, it is in the organisation's interest that employees should be well-informed about its economic circumstances. Employees cannot be expected to adopt a realistic approach to pay rises or to organisational change if there has been no information or explanation of relevant financial and market factors.

Information media

It should be evident that no single method of communication will suffice. What the organisation requires is an open culture, a transparency of activity, in which a wide variety of communication methods and media combine to keep everyone, at all times, well informed.

Before considering these methods individually, there is an important general principle to grasp: the need for consistency between formal and informal communication modes. Even without any formal channels, information about the organisation will flow. Managers will talk to their staff, office gossip will flourish and reinforce organisational mythology, and employees will pick up news items from the local or trade press and from seeing internal documents.

Suppose a formal strategy is adopted, including the

launch of a house journal. If the message and style of this strategy is in conflict with the general impression created by the informal communication networks, the formal element is likely to be discredited as mere organisational propaganda. To be effective an information strategy has to embrace or influence the informal element.

The most commonly-used means of transmitting information include:

- informal contacts
- briefing groups
- notices
- letters to employees
- house journals
- mass meetings
- annual employee reports.

Informal contacts

Managers should be encouraged to use their everyday working contacts with staff as one means of passing on information, but it needs to be accurate and consistent with any formal information briefing or messages. So the first step may well need to be a review of how managers obtain information about the organisation and of the quality of this data. At the level of the individual job, almost the whole of the information process lies with the manager or supervisor. Only at this level can the role and significance of any one job be explained, and explanations given for new instructions or requirements. Informally, this explanatory approach should be promoted as a matter of management style: saying why something has to be done as well as issuing instructions. Formally, one function of an appraisal scheme is to ensure that each employee understands the purpose of the job and the need for certain standards to be achieved.

Briefing groups

The concept of briefing groups, in which managers or supervisors talk regularly to their work groups, stems partly from recognition of the importance of consistency of information throughout the organisation. Through a cascade system, each level in the organisation briefs the next with information which top management wishes to be disseminated to the whole workforce. Part of the briefing group process thus consists of giving briefing managers notes on key issues to ensure that information is not distorted by word of mouth as it cascades through the organisation. To this each manager adds information specific to the work group, while the whole network also provides a channel of communication back up the organisation as managers relay to their seniors questions raised by their briefing groups.

Notices

Some managers rely far too much on the use of notice boards for formal company announcements and messages. Dull-looking badly-worded typed announcements pinned carelessly among a clutter of dog-eared and out-of-date notices are not a good way of attracting attention for relaying important messages. The impact of notices can, however, be improved by

- using plain English principles when drafting them
- using modern reprographics, including colour and images, to make the notice visually interesting

■ frequent weeding of notice boards to take down outdated or unofficial material.

Letters to employees

The occasional use of letters to every employee can be a useful way of drawing attention to an issue of major importance or explaining a matter of considerable interest or concern. It is probably not a good method to use on a routine basis because it then loses its impact and may undermine the role of managers in relaying organisational information through briefing groups. When used, the wording is extremely important if misunderstanding or resentment is to be avoided. Managers should also be briefed in advance so that they can deal immediately with employee questions and reactions.

House journals

The production of a house journal is not something to be embarked upon lightly or in an amateur fashion, and needs a chapter in itself (see Chapter 16) to explain adequately. But among the main points to consider are:

■ the need to distinguish between information for employees and material designed for external public relations
■ the style of journal best suited to the needs and style of the organisation – the options ranging from a glossy publication with high-quality graphic design to a popular tabloid type news-sheet
■ the frequency of publication, which will be determined by the volume and rapidity of activity and change within the organisation
■ the essential requirement for the publication to

have credibility among the workforce – something which will not be achieved if it is seen as a closely controlled organisational mouthpiece subject to detailed managerial censorship

▪ the need to deal with serious issues seriously, and to avoid an exclusive focus on trivia and social events.

A well-produced journal which deals with important issues clearly and frankly, can play a major part in an effective information strategy.

Mass meetings

There is a role, on occasion, for the mass meeting of all or of large groups of the staff, addressed by top management. Some companies make this an annual event to explain each year's results – a presentation much improved by the use of visual aids or videos. Mass meetings may also help in the explanation of major organisational change, although because it is not possible to deal adequately with questions and comments, managers need prior briefing so that they can deal with employee reaction in smaller follow-up groups.

Annual employee reports

An increasing number of companies produce an annual employee report in parallel with the annual shareholders' report. Some of the material is common to both types of report, but the employees' report can deal in more detail with internal issues and highlight specific employee achievements.

Further reading

1 *Practical Participation and Involvement* series. London, Institute of Personnel Management, 1981/2.

2 BLAKSTAD M. *and* COOPER A. *The Communicating Organisation*. London, Institute of Personnel and Development, 1995.

16   House journals

In recent years there has been a growing awareness of the need for employees to be well-informed about the aims and activities of their organisations. Mission statements and lists of core values have little impact unless they are communicated and explained to the whole workforce in ways which relate to everyday working experience. Qualities such as commitment, innovation or customer care depend on employees' knowing what their organisation considers important and how each work activity fits into the total picture. So effective communication becomes a vital element in the successful management of the human resource.

There are, of course, many means of communication: briefing groups, notices and company video are just some of the best known. But one of the most effective – if it is done well – is the staff magazine or house journal. Its particular advantages are that:

  ▪ It can go directly to each employee – something difficult to guarantee for some of the other methods.
  ▪ It ensures that all employees receive the same information at the same time, and so helps to build a consistent corporate identity.

It is often taken home, so its impact goes beyond the workplace.

It may be kept and read over a significant time period, thus having a longer-term impact than the transient spoken word.

On the down side, the wrong type of house journal for its readership may do more than just waste the money spent on its production. A journal with a style and content inconsistent with the reality of employees' daily experience will fuel cynicism and sap morale. Making a success of a house journal therefore requires careful attention to the readership, the journal's objectives, the range of its content, the frequency of publication, style, format and cost, and how it is to be produced.

Readership

All publications need to be tailored to their target readership. The reading habits of most highly-qualified professionals vary from those of the majority of shop-floor personnel, and these differences need to be reflected to some degree in the house journal. This is relatively easy if there is a homogeneous workforce, although examples could be quoted of tabloid news-sheets written in idiot-speak being issued to staff whose daily reading is the *Guardian* or *The Independent*. So the first step, even with a single-occupation workforce, is to consider the nature of the readership. There is more of a problem with a varied workforce, perhaps with PhD research staff at one end of the spectrum and stores labourers at the other.

In reaching a position between the professional glossy and the popular tabloid, two points can be borne in mind: do not underestimate the intelligence of so-called unskilled employees and their potential interest in their organisation's plans, products and processes; and do not assume that the interests of highly-qualified professionals are limited to the technicalities of their own work or to business theory. They too enjoy human interest stories, as well as needing a more comprehensive picture of the organisation than they may obtain from the perspective of their particular functions.

Objectives

What does the organisation wish to achieve from the production of a house journal? The objective may be seen in general terms as being to improve employees' knowledge of, and interest in, the organisation. But to ensure an effectively focused journal more specific aims are needed. Some possible objectives are:

- to promote understanding and commitment to the organisation's core values
- to generate cross-functional collaboration by explaining the part each function plays in the operation of the organisation as a whole
- to provide a channel of communication to all employees for information about company policies, procedures and rules
- to support employee training by providing explanations of the organisation's processes
- to generate a sense of fun and excitement within the working environment.

Other objectives could be suggested; the key point is that each organisation should define its own aims. Unless this is done, the journal risks a lack of coherence and consistency.

Content

The journal's objectives will largely determine its range of content. So an emphasis on factual information will indicate a need for articles about the organisation's products, services and processes. A concern to promote certain core values will be met by stories of how particular sections or individuals have translated these values into practical action. An objective of giving the organisation a human face will require personal profiles of managers and achievers and a search for human stories behind the organisation's results.

Each objective needs to be taken in turn and the question asked: What type of news and features will best meet this aim? There is also one major point of principle – whatever the subject matter, it should be honestly presented and include bad as well as good news. House journals which exaggerate success, or ignore major failures or other matters which are worrying the workforce, rapidly lose credibility. The house journal provides an opportunity to correct inaccurate grapevine rumours and to show that management recognises the concerns employees have for the well-being of their organisation.

Frequency

The objectives and content will have an influence on the journal's frequency of issue. If the main function is news, a quarterly will be wholly inappropriate. News by definition is information which is new – there are few company events of any significance which do not become known by one means or another within a very short time after they have occurred.

A quarterly can be a useful medium for explanations of trends, background data about major events and messages about the future. It is no place for 'Welcome back to Jill Bloggs who has just returned from maternity leave', when she has been back at work for weeks. A monthly is probably the lowest frequency for any sort of news coverage, and then only as a section within a wider range of subject matter. Some organisations which aim to provide both an up-to-date news service and in-depth information about general company affairs use two media: a simple weekly news-sheet and a more solid or glossy quarterly.

Costs may prevent many organisations from adopting this approach, and in this case the frequency of a single journal must be governed by its primary objectives. A modestly-sized news-sheet produced fairly frequently is often more effective than the same volume of material in a journal produced only three or four times a year.

Style, format and cost

Style is comprised of the tone or quality of writing and the journal's appearance – particularly its imagery and graphic design. House journals produced by amateurs commonly display two faults. Firstly, they adopt a tone of enforced jollity in their writing style. Almost every item is treated in a light-hearted fashion, with feeble attempts at humorous headlines. Secondly, particularly if the journal is produced by an in-house desktop publishing system, the layout is fussy, with far too many variations of typeface and no design coherence.

The ability to write clearly, simply and in a style which matches a particular readership is not widely distributed. It is not a skill available within all personnel departments – although it would be helpful if it were. It should not be assumed, either, that marketing staff have it. House journals produced by marketing departments usually fall into the trap of adopting a promotional style which employees dislike. The necessary skills may well lie within the press and information unit (if one exists), but may need to be bought in, either through recruitment or by the use of a specialist consultancy. A similar point applies to layout, artwork and typographic design, on which it is essential to obtain professional advice if the journal is to have an effective visual impact.

The journal's format also needs to be consistent with its aims and style. Should it be a simple A4 news-sheet, a tabloid, a saddle-stitched monthly or quarterly? Should it be in black and white, or use spot or full colour? What quality of paper should be used? What should be its title and masthead? All these points need thorough consideration and professional advice, together with their cost implications.

Costs are obviously influenced by the journal's size (dimensions and pagination), paper quality, use of colour, numbers of copies to be printed, and issue frequency. It is also worth bearing in mind three other factors:

- If the material can be supplied to the printer on disk or by e-mail, rather than on hard copy, it will reduce production costs.
- There are the sometimes hidden costs of staff time to consider, particularly if the journal is produced

as a part-time or occasional activity alongside other work. The time necessary to produce an effective house journal is often gravely underestimated. Writing articles, commissioning, chasing and editing contributors' copy, planning layouts, preparing the material for printing, and checking and correcting proofs are not tasks for the already busy personnel manager who wishes to produce a journal of any quality.

■ Legal costs can arise with regard to such matters as libel and copyright (or insurance against such risks) – another reason for obtaining professional advice.

How the journal is produced

There are many different ways in which a journal can be produced. It may be an in-house operation as part of a wider function (eg within a press or personnel department), or a dedicated operation with a full-time company editor who should be a professional journalist with access to the necessary specialist design and production expertise.

Then there are operations using some in-house resources but directed by a professional freelance editor, and those which use a specialist design and printing company while producing all copy internally. Finally, you can use a specialist consultancy or publication company for the whole operation. The best of these organisations are generally those specialising in the design and production of house journals rather than generalist publishers or marketing-oriented consultancies. Lists can be obtained from the British Association of Industrial Editors.

There is no one best way which applies to everyone. The right solution for each organisation depends on the type and frequency of journal it decides to produce and whether in-house skills and resources can be made available. One thing is certain: to compromise on professionalism is to risk spending money on an amateur production which will not achieve the desired objectives and may actually damage employee relations.

Further information

BLAKSTAD M. *and* COOPER A. *The Communicating Organisation.* London, Institute of Personnel and Development, 1995.

Improving performance

17   Teambuilding

One feature of flexible organisations is an emphasis on teamworking, both as a standard work system and for handling specific projects.

Team selection can have a major influence on organisational performance. The success of multi-skilled work groups depends heavily on their operating within a collaborative team culture. How well a project team completes its task is similarly influenced by its members' abilities to establish an effective team process.

The characteristics of an effective team are:

- There is a common sense of purpose and a clear understanding of the team's objectives.
- The team has, or can obtain, all the resources it needs to achieve its objectives.
- Among the team members there is the range of skills and know-how needed to deal effectively with the team's tasks.
- There is also a range of team types within the team – ie team members have different aptitudes for the various team roles required for effective teamworking.

■ Team members have respect for each other, both as individuals and for the contribution each makes to the team's performance.

It is evident from these features that there are two broad requirements in selecting the members of a team: the team should include the range of specialist or technical expertise needed for tasks involved; and its members should have a variety of personal styles in order to fill the different roles that are involved in effective team-working.

Although the precise nature of the expertise needed in each team is determined by the work, there are two points that are relevant to almost all teams, regardless of their precise specialist requirements. The first is that team membership should be determined solely by the nature of the expertise that the tasks require. Members should be selected for their know-how, and not for seniority or any other criteria related to status.

It is not unusual for this to result in a team which includes a range of members of varying status, and for some of the most junior members to be the best informed on certain aspects of the issue at hand. An example might be a project team set up to examine a customer complaints procedure which includes representatives of the staff to whom customers first bring complaints, as well as more senior personnel who are concerned with policy considerations. The team itself must operate without regard to status – teams are essentially non-hierarchical.

The second point is that many project teams benefit from having members drawn from a wide range of interests. Organisations which have traditionally operated with very clearly defined functional or professional boundaries sometimes fail to secure the benefits of full cross-functional teamworking. They may use a team approach but restrict team membership to staff who traditionally 'own' the subjects under discussion.

Many IT projects have failed when the teams concerned have consisted entirely of IT specialists, with the result that inadequate attention is given to the views and needs of IT users. The question to ask is 'Who has ideas or information that will help the team to succeed?' not 'Who is currently responsible for the issue to be addressed?'

Some organisations are now extending the principle of broadly-based project team membership beyond the organisation's own employees. Companies may invite customers or suppliers to join teams. Some local authorities are including tenants, leisure centre users and local business people in teams that review or monitor aspects of housing, leisure services or economic development.

However, the fact that a team's membership has all the necessary knowledge and expertise does not guarantee its success. Teams fail if their members cannot work together effectively, and this is a function of personality and attitude, not of specialist know-how. It is a serious mistake to assume there is a single type of team person. What is needed is a mix of types. It is only necessary to consider the dynamics of a team in which all the members want to be team leader to see how ineffective a team made up of a single type of person would be. The only characteristic team members must have in common is a willingness to work together.

The pioneering research on team performance and team types was carried out by Dr Meredith Belbin at the

Administrative Staff College at Henley. Belbin has gone on to produce one of the most widely-used questionnaires for team selection and team training, and his analysis of team typology forms the basis for almost all work in this field.

The initial assumption was that a team composed of managers who scored the highest on a mental ability test would produce the best team results. In practice these teams of clever people generally performed very badly. They were characterised by destructive debate, by individual members' unwillingness to consider other members' views, and by a lack of coherence in their solutions.

Belbin moved on to see if there was one particular type or style of team member common to all the successful teams. Such team members were practical, tolerant towards others, tough-minded, conservative, and had a good self-image. Belbin labelled them 'company workers'. But when teams were formed consisting entirely of company workers, team performance was poor. These teams were characterised by good organisation and effort, but were inflexible and lacking in ideas.

From experiments of this kind Belbin evolved the concept of team typology, and eventually identified nine different team types. This does not imply that the ideal team size is nine, although there is ample evidence to indicate that a good team needs to include several types. Two types appear to be particularly helpful in project teams in addition to company workers (now described by Belbin as *'implementers'*):

- 'co-ordinators' – not necessarily the brightest or most creative in the group, but good in a chairing role:

they are respected by the team, clarify its goals, and promote decision-making

- 'plants' – clever, innovative and creative people: they are the ideas people, good at tackling difficult problems, although their solutions may require careful assessment for their practicability.

Putting these three types together (plant, implementer and co-ordinator) gives a combination of bright ideas, practicality and direction. However, the make-up of any particular team should take account both of its optimum size and the specific characteristics of its tasks. Team size needs to be sufficient to incorporate the requisite range of expertise and representation of interests, although teams of more than about eight people may find it difficult to ensure every team member's participation.

If for technical or representational reasons it is necessary to form a very large team, it is generally advisable to divide its work between smaller sub-groups; the whole team should meet mainly to review and co-ordinate overall progress.

The nature of the team's tasks should also influence the typology of its membership. If the issues and aims are not particularly complex and the requirement is for a fast-moving implementation plan, the need for a plant diminishes. In this case a dynamic, challenging type ('shaper' in Belbin's terminology) may have a leading role. If the tasks require careful, detailed scrutiny and evaluation, the 'monitor-evaluator' (serious, strategic, discerning) and 'completer' (painstaking, conscientious) come into their own.

A 'resource investigator' (enthusiastic, exploratory) will

assist any team which needs an outgoing member who is good at finding external contacts and sources of support. And if it is known that there are likely to be personal tensions between some of these team members, the presence of a friendly *'teamworker'* (mild, perceptive, accommodating) will help to reduce friction.

Whatever method is used to assess potential team behaviour, it is important to recognise that individuals rarely fall neatly into Belbin-type categories. The plant may also have strong shaper characteristics, or the team-worker may also be a completer. In addition, some people – who may be the most effective team members of all – have an ability to adopt different roles as circumstances require. Team selection requires shrewd judgement: it is not a mechanical process.

Given this qualification, there are several ways of identifying potential team members' characteristics. One is simply to consider the evidence of strengths and weaknesses, as exhibited in previous team situations. Previous team leaders can be asked to describe their team members' team behaviours. There may also be clues in employees' performance appraisal records.

There may, however, be insufficient evidence of this type, or doubts about the ability of team leaders to make this kind of assessment objectively. Some form of testing is then useful. Most general personality questionnaires – such as the OPQ, Myers Briggs or 16PF – can provide useful indications of likely team behaviour. For those organisations wishing to apply the specific Belbin approach, Belbin Associates has developed a test instrument called Interface IV which can be used to identify team aptitudes. Unlike most personality tests this can include the completion of a questionnaire by one or more observers of test subjects, as well as a self-completed questionnaire.

The Belbin typology is not the only approach to team selection. At recent IPD conferences in Harrogate there have been 30 or more exhibitors offering various forms of team development training, and a number of these have their own team-type classifications. Organisations should research these sources and decide for themselves which approach best meets their needs.

This chapter has given prominence to the Belbin approach simply because of the extent to which it is based on published research and because it is widely accepted as having focused attention on the importance of different team roles.

Further information

1 BELBIN M. R. *Management Teams: Why they succeed or fail.* London, Butterworth Heinemann, 1981.

2 Interface IV: Belbin Associates, The Burleigh Business Centre, 52 Burleigh Street, Cambridge CB1 1DJ (01223 464 123).

3 HARDINGHAM A. *and* ROYAL J. *Pulling Together: Teamwork in practice.* London, Institute of Personnel and Development, 1994.

4 HARDINGHAM A. *Working in Teams.* London, Institute of Personnel and Development 1996.

18 Setting performance objectives

The setting of performance objectives has become a major element in employee management for at least three related reasons. Firstly, the earlier use of merit-rating – based on very generalised and subjective criteria – has been largely replaced by performance assessments against far more specific, often quantified, targets or standards. Secondly, the growth in performance-related pay requires appraisal systems in which performance ratings are based on achievements against objectives. Thirdly, performance management systems (not necessarily linked to pay) have been widely introduced which involve the identification of a hierarchy of objectives, beginning with corporate aims, and eventually lead to a set of objectives specific to each employee.

The setting of objectives serves two main functions: to ensure that everyone in the organisation is working towards the same overall goals, and to provide individual direction. People work best when they know what their jobs are there for, the standards to be achieved, and how they are performing against these objectives.

Objective-setting can, however, damage staff morale if targets are unrealistic or do not cover important aspects of the work. An effective system has four principal characteristics.

1 Individual employees' objectives will be related to the aims and priorities of the organisation and of the section in which the employee works, and form a co-ordinated whole. Where appropriate, team objectives will be adopted.
2 Objectives will be evolved jointly between each individual and his or her manager – not imposed without discussion.
3 Objectives will be reasonable aspirations for competent people to achieve, but will not be so readily achievable as to discredit the system. They will also be mainly dependent on the performance of the individual. Any influencing factors outside the employee's control will be identified, and they will be capable of measurement or systematic assessment.
4 If set annually, objectives will be adjusted in the course of the year in the light of unforeseen changes.

Performance measurement

The aspect which many employees and managers find most difficult – particularly in white-collar and service jobs – is identifying the performance measures. Yet there is little point in setting objectives which are not assessable by largely objective criteria. This is not to say that the only meaningful objectives are those which can be assessed by direct financial or quantitative measurements. Many jobs (including personnel work) have important qualitative requirements which necessitate other forms of assessment. The important point is that these assessments should be rational, systematic and stable over time so that trends can be reliably tracked. If in some cases the assessment has to be subjective opinion, it should be obtained in a thorough, repeatable and systematic way.

Although performance measures ought to be very specific to each job, they can be categorised, starting with the most directly quantified and going on to more qualitative indicators. These include:

- direct financial indices (such as product or service unit costs, sales volumes, profits)
- other direct quantitative measures (such as numbers of units of production, numbers of customers or client contacts)
- ratios (for example, errors per thousand transactions, sales per hundred customer contacts, labour turnover or absence ratios)
- time factors (particularly durations and deadlines, such as average time to complete a transaction, target dates for completion of projects, waiting times)
- judgemental scales (the rating of opinions or assessments, as used in market research and attitude surveys).

Descriptive opinions (for example, by customers or senior managers) are the most subjective form of assessment but may be acceptable where no more direct form of measurement is possible, provided the opinions are well-informed and, if challenged, can be substantiated by evidence.

Types of objectives

Objectives can be described within two sets of dimensions: task-related/personal competence, and short-term/standing.

Task-related objectives are those concerned with outputs and quality and the achievement of specific tasks or projects. Two examples might be the reduction of an error rate to 1 in 10,000 by 1 June and the achievement of 5 per cent improvement in client satisfaction ratings by the end of 1999.

Personal competence objectives are concerned with improving an individual employee's knowledge or skill. Examples of this could be the gaining of a sound working knowledge of the use of computerised spreadsheets before the next annual review and improving report-writing skills to a standard suitable for major client presentations by, say, the end of July.

Short-term objectives deal with matters requiring one-off action or non-repetitive issues, such as completion of the office relocation programme, within budget, by 30 September or the taking up of the OU Competent Manager course in November.

Standing objectives are concerned with permanent or ongoing features of the job and may be expressed in terms such as maintaining a level of customer satisfaction in which complaints do not exceed 1 in 1,000 transactions or ensuring that administration costs are kept to no more than 5 per cent of direct costs. The figures may be changed occasionally, but the underlying objectives (eg customer satisfaction, low overheads) are standing features of the job.

Confusion may exist about the difference between objectives and action plans. Some performance management systems make a clear distinction, while others combine these two features. Where a distinction is made, the objective will identify the goal and an action plan will then specify how that goal is to be achieved. As an example, if the objective is to reduce staffing costs by 10 per cent by October, the action plan might be the amalgamation of the word-processing and reprographics sections to reduce total staff by five.

Alternatively, the objective may either omit any planned action because how it is to be achieved is left to the initiative of the jobholder, or it may be combined with the agreed action plan. If, for example, the objective is to increase the number of daily telephone contacts with customers by 15 per cent, the action plan could include the transferring of record-sheet analysis from telesales staff to the administrative section.

Agreeing objectives

How objectives are determined is almost as important as their content, the aim being to achieve employees' full commitment to their individual goals. Objective-setting is consequently most effective when it is done by discussion between manager and employee. This discussion, together with a review of performance to date against previous objectives, should form the major part of the periodic appraisal meeting.

Employees should receive training in the concepts and

practice of performance management, including advice on thinking about their objectives in advance of the appraisal discussion and bringing proposals for new or amended objectives to the meeting. The job description, or schedule of principal accountabilities, can be used as a checklist of aspects of the job which may require attention.

Asked, in effect, to set their own objectives and standards, many people will suggest more ambitious targets than their managers might think appropriate to impose. Indeed, managers may need to advise staff against committing themselves to too many or too difficult objectives. Agreed objectives should be challenging but achievable.

Managers must ensure that the objectives of different employees do not conflict. Very few jobs are wholly self-contained, and new action for one employee may require supportive action by another or need modification to fit other employees' objectives. It is also important that the organisation's and section's corporate objectives are reflected in those of individual employees.

The outcome of an appraisal discussion should include a new or revised schedule of objectives, agreed between manager and employee. Each objective should have either a deadline for achievement or be understood as being subject to review at the time of the next appraisal.

Objective-setting will fail, however, if it is left as a once-a-year exercise. The principle of working towards defined goals needs to be part of an ongoing system of management, and objectives agreed at an annual appraisal may have to be modified or even scrapped as the year progresses and unforeseen circumstances arise. The unexpected availability of a new product or service may thus provide an opportunity for raising standards. New business developments or legislation may necessitate previously unplanned action, requiring time and effort which can be found only by changing current deadlines. The unpredictability of organisational life is no argument for abandoning objective-setting: it merely emphasises the need for objectives to be kept under continuous review.

A periodic stock-take

The formal periodic appraisal then becomes a stock-take and should address these questions:

- What objectives did we agree last time which have been achieved?
- Which are still valid but have not yet been achieved?
- Why, and what action is now needed to achieve them?
- What new objectives have been agreed since the last review?
- What progress has been made towards meeting these new or modified objectives – and are any new action plans needed?
- Do any current objectives need modification?
- What new objectives and action plans should now be agreed?

Further reading

1 ARMSTRONG M. and BARON A. Performance Management: The new realities. London, Institute of Personnel and Development, 1998.

2 WALTERS M. *The Performance Management Handbook.* London, Institute of Personnel and Development, 1995. 3 GILLEN T. *The Appraisal Discussion.* London, Institute of Personnel and Development, 1995.

19   Conducting appraisals

Appraisal schemes are in all but universal use throughout the private and public sectors, although the style or emphasis in these schemes varies considerably between different organisations. The two main variants have been a bias towards staff development – the identification of employees' training and career needs, and a primary emphasis on improving job performance. The performance approach can then be subdivided into schemes which link appraisal directly with decisions about performance payments and those which keep appraisal separate from pay.

Whatever their emphasis, all schemes have at their core periodic (usually annual) discussions between each employee and his or her manager, and to a large extent schemes fail or succeed depending on the skill with which these discussions are conducted. Many managers have difficulty with appraisal. They may see it as an artificial process imposed by top management or, worse, by the personnel department. Even when they intellectually accept its potential value, they may lack the practical skills or confidence to handle the process effectively. In short, managers need guidance, and in many organisations it falls to the personnel manager to provide it.

Appraisal is essentially a matter of being systematic about some commonsense elements of naturally good management. There are no artificial or specialist tricks or techniques, and managers should not be expected to behave out of character.

The basic principle can be described almost in words of one syllable: staff work best when they know what they have to do, how well they have to do it, and how well they are thought to have done, so they need to talk with their managers at least once a year about it, and their managers need to take their staff's views into account when they set work goals and decide who needs what training.

For appraisals to be effective, both parties must prepare for the discussion. Adequate time must be set aside for the discussion, and it must be held in a quiet environment, free from interruptions. The discussion has to follow a logical sequence and involve an interchange of views – appraisal is a two-way process, not an inquisition or exposition by the manager. The emphasis should be on positive comment and action – it should not comprise a negative post-mortem of past faults – and the primary outcome should be an agreed schedule of planned, constructive action.

Before an appraisal meeting, both parties need to give thought to what they wish to discuss and consider how best to raise these issues. Organisations often train managers in the appraisal process and stress the importance of preparation but do not give similar guidance to the appraisees. Yet one of the most important features of appraisal is the opportunity it provides for employees to make comments and suggestions to their managers and to discuss these in a situation unhampered by the time pressures of the normal work environment.

In some schemes employees complete their own comprehensive self-assessments before the appraisal, and these form the basis for the discussion. Assessments by peers and subordinates provide material for discussion for those organisations operating 360-degree appraisal systems. But whatever the formal sources of information and documentation, employees should always be advised to bring a note with them of the key points they want to talk about – just as managers need to be clear about their priority issues for discussion.

Appraisals tend to take longer than managers originally expect. Unless adequate time is set aside, the very important last stages will be rushed, or the whole discussion will be too superficial. Except for simple jobs which are being well done by employees with no particular training or career interests, one-and-a-half hours is not too long to set aside. Complex managerial or professional jobs, with significant employee developmental needs and a requirement to identify and agree new performance targets, may well take much longer. Rushed appraisals are worse than useless.

It is also essential to ensure a reasonably quiet location, free from telephone interruptions and chance callers. This rules out the use of an open-plan office, or conducting appraisals over a restaurant lunch.

This chapter uses the term 'appraisal discussion' rather than the more common 'appraisal interview' in order to emphasis the two-way nature of the process. This does not imply an unstructured conversation: the discussion needs to follow a logical sequence. Most experienced appraisers prefer first to review past performance and then to consider the aims and action for the next review period. Similarly, when the appraisal system is comprehensive it seems best to deal with immediate job performance first, followed by discussion of the longer-term training or career development issues.

Two documents may be helpful in addition to any pre-completed assessments: the job description, which can serve as a checklist to ensure that all aspects of the work have been considered and to agree any necessary revisions to the description, and the record of the previous appraisal – particularly the targets and action plans – which can provide a good starting-point ('This is what we agreed to do last time; what have we actually achieved?').

Some appraisers use the following outline to ensure that the discussion covers the necessary ground and ends on a positive note:

1   a reminder of the purpose of the discussion
2   a brief exchange in which each party itemises the key points they want to discuss – setting the agenda
3   a point-by-point examination of the results of the aims and action agreed at the last review
    and/or
4   a check against each element in the job description, considering which aspects have gone well and which less well, and why

5   discussion and agreement on the job-performance
    aims for the next review period
6   a similar discussion on the employee's
    developmental objectives
7   agreement on the action each needs to take, by
    when, to achieve the performance and
    developmental objectives
8   a brief 'any other business' exchange in which each
    can raise any matters not yet dealt with
9   a check that there is mutual understanding of the
    key points and action plans.

There is more to appraisal than managers' giving direction and guidance to their staff. Managers too can learn from the process – provided they encourage staff to use the opportunity of the appraisal discussion to raise issues of interest or concern. One way of doing this is to begin the appraisal by asking the employee to comment on achievements and problems during the review period, rather than the manager's immediately giving his or her views.

The discussion techniques are somewhat similar to those of selection interviewing. The manager's aim should be to do less talking than the appraisee, using open-ended questions which require a narrative answer, or following any managerial statement with a question such as 'What do you feel about that?'

The employee should also be given an opening to tell the appraiser about matters the manager should address. Questions to the appraisee which can result in very enlightening comments are: 'Is there anything about the way I am doing my job as a manager which makes your job more difficult?' 'Is there anything I might do to make it easier for you to meet your targets?' Wise managers use appraisal to discover things about their own performance.

There is a danger that employees will approach an appraisal discussion with trepidation, fearing it will be little more than a fault-finding exercise. Alternatively, they may be cynical about its value because they know (or detect) that their managers do not consider it an important activity but rather a chore to be got through as quickly as possible. Having an appraisal scheme that has acquired this kind of reputation is worse than not having one at all: appraisal is worth doing only if the managers involved believe in it and handle it in a positive, constructive manner.

This is not to say that failure to achieve targets or other difficulties should not be discussed. Appraisal is the opportunity for these to be carefully considered within the context of the whole job. But in looking at failure the question should be 'What can we learn from this?', not 'Who was to blame?'

The discussion should result in an agreed programme of action, not just an agreed set of conclusions about past performance. It helps to consider action plans as having four dimensions:

- action to be initiated by the employee
- action to be initiated by the manager or by some other person, such as the personnel officer
- work-oriented action – for example, a change in work routines
- employee-oriented action – for example, additional training, a self-study programme.

Finally, action plans need target implementation and completion deadlines so that progress can be monitored as part of the ongoing process of informal appraisal which characterises the style of effective managers. Action plans give the answers to the question 'To achieve what we have agreed, who is to do what by when?'

Further reading

1 GILLEN T. *The Appraisal Discussion*. London, Institute of Personnel and Development, 1995.
2 FLETCHER C. *Appraisal: Routes to improved performance*. 2nd edn. London, Institute of Personnel and Development, 1997.

20   Employee counselling

How well people work is influenced by more than just their level of training or qualifications, or the impact of motivators such as performance-related pay. The ability of an employee to sustain interest and concentration, to display care and imagination, or to maintain a high level of courtesy to customers, is affected by personal issues which are not addressed by the formalities of reward or disciplinary systems. Case law is also developing which indicates that employers may be liable for the effects of ignoring employees' foreseeable mental problems caused by work-based stress.

There are many work-based symptoms of personal problems which affect employees' attitudes and so may lie behind inadequate performance or unsatisfactory conduct. These may include inattention to important detail; rows with colleagues which are out of proportion to the issues involved; insensitivity to the feelings of fellow employees or the public; failure to communicate; erratic performance; sickness absences; frequent resort to the grievance procedure for relatively minor matters;

obsessive attention to detail; and 'workaholism' and unusual reluctance to delegate.

Of course, not all such behaviour is attributable to personal stress. Some may indicate a mismatch between the employee's ability or interest and the nature and demands of the job. A high standard of selection and training and, at times, the judicious use of disciplinary action will greatly reduce the extent of poor performance or unsatisfactory conduct. But in even the best-managed workforce there will still be cases in which the basic problems are personal. In recent years there has been a growing recognition among employers that the incidence and effect of such problems is greater than a casual view would indicate. More positively, there has also been a realisation that there is something the employer can do about it by providing counselling.

Before deciding what counselling facilities might be provided and how, it is necessary to recognise the wide range of factors which may lead to employee stress. It is too simple to think of personal stress and counselling as being concerned almost wholly with one issue, such as relationship problems. Many factors may be involved, and an effective counselling service needs to have the ability to identify the many sources of possible problems and the expertise to deal with them.

Stress factors can be either work-based or external to work. Work-based factors can include:

- rumours of redundancies
- changes in job content or the working environment
- sexual or racial harassment
- industrial disputes

- customer behaviour and complaints
- high-pressure working
- insufficient or uninteresting work
- disciplinary action
- personality clashes with management or colleagues
- impending or enforced retirement.

Factors external to work can include:

- personal financial worries
- bereavement
- marital and relationship problems
- stressful commuting
- inadequate housing
- health problems
- childcare problems and care for elderly relatives
- substance abuse.

Counselling should not be thought of in terms either of solving other people's problems or of being merely a means of showing sympathy. The essence of effective counselling is an ability to help people under stress identify for themselves what the real issues are and to support them in the decisions they take to ease or resolve their problems. An approach in which the counsellor takes over and makes all the decisions may well make the problem worse by confirming a person's lack of self-esteem and leading to undue dependence on the counsellor. At the other extreme, if counselling is limited to exuding sympathy it may do little more than reinforce a person's sense of unhappiness or inadequacy.

Counselling requires a high level of sensitivity and skill, and a wide knowledge of the various agencies and specialist organisations which can provide practical assistance for specific personal problems. That does not mean, however, that counselling should be provided only by fully trained professional counsellors.

The provision of counselling support can be considered at four levels: supervisory and management staff, personnel staff, specialist in-house counsellors, and external counselling services.

Supervisors and managers

Supervisors are often the first to notice the symptoms of employee stress, even if they do not initially recognise them as indicating a possible counselling need. There is therefore a strong case for including a counselling module in any supervisory or management training programme. The aim is not to turn managers into full-blown counsellors but rather to ensure that they are aware of the possibility that many performance and conduct problems have an origin in personal stress. The training should also show how to handle the initial discussion about work or personal problems and explain where the employee may be directed to obtain further assistance.

Personnel staff

Personnel professionals may be the first point of contact for employees with personal problems, particularly if these are concerned with employees' relationships with their managers. In the absence of a specialist in-house service, the generalist personnel officer is commonly expected to act as a welfare officer – a role which has, perhaps, been undervalued in recent years.

Personnel staff can play a valuable part in reducing

the adverse impact of employee stress on organisational performance if they have the skills – developed by training – to go further in the counselling process than line managers, and if they have available comprehensive information about external sources of specialist assistance.

In-house services

Many organisations with occupational health units expect their nurses and doctors to provide stress counselling, although this tends to be medically biased and may not cover important aspects such as debt or redundancy counselling. Large organisations may be able to justify the cost of establishing specialist in-house services, staffed by professionally-trained counsellors.

There are several issues to resolve in setting up such a service. First, their organisational setting: to whom should they be accountable? Normally it is the personnel manager, but some would argue that to obtain maximum credibility counsellors need to be seen by staff as an independent unit. The second issue is confidentiality. It is essential that staff have total confidence in the service and a clear understanding about the extent to which the counsellor may inform management of issues raised by employees. Even the physical location of the service can affect staff perceptions.

Finally, there is control and budgeting: how is the effectiveness of the service to be assessed and decisions made about its scale and expenditure? Total confidentiality makes it difficult for the service to report its activities, but anonymous monitoring is necessary if a reasonable degree of control or oversight is to be maintained.

External services

Broadly speaking, there are two kinds of external counselling services: specialist and generalist. The most widely-used specialists are probably outplacement consultancies, which primarily provide redundancy counselling. There are many other specialist agencies dealing with such topics as careers advice, substance abuse, marriage guidance and debt counselling. These all depend on the managers or personnel staff, together with the employees concerned, to make the right diagnosis of the problem and so to select the appropriate agency.

A broader alternative is to contract with an external generalist agency for the provision of a comprehensive counselling service – often termed an employee assistance programme. This may involve a fixed fee, fees for each case, or a combination of a retainer plus case fees.

Among the most important issues to consider in addition to the service's professional *bona fides* are whether the agency understands the culture of the client organisation sufficiently well to identify work-based causes of employee problems; whether employees can seek counselling without first obtaining permission – too rigorous a vetting system will undermine the service, too open-ended an approach may result in unacceptable costs; and what information or monitoring data the agency should provide to ensure the client organisation of its cost-effectiveness.

Whatever approach is followed, none will be effective unless top management is committed to the value of counselling, and managers generally (with personnel staff) have at least a basic understanding of its purpose and methods. To introduce a counselling service only for management to refuse to consider many of the work-based issues which it is likely to spotlight is probably worse than not having the service at all.

Further information

1 British Association for Counselling: 1 Regent Place, Rugby, CV21 2PJ (01766 550899).

2 SUMMERFIELD J. *and* VAN OUDTSHOORN L. *Counselling in the Workplace*. London, Institute of Personnel and Development, 1995.

3 COOPER C. *and* EARNSHAW J. *Stress and Employer Liability*. London, Institute of Personnel and Development, 1996.

21   Controlling absence

As a result of staff absence, organisations annually lose anything from two to as many as 15 days per employee. National statistics show that the average working time lost is 3.7 per cent, or about eight and a half days a year, and that manual employees take significantly more sick leave than non-manual staff. Any employer who fails to introduce positive measures to reduce absence is missing a major opportunity to improve efficiency.

The starting-point for any absence reduction programme is to define the types of absence that need to be addressed and to ensure that cases are being recorded. Most schemes require attendance targets and benchmarking exercises, and these depend on the availability of accurate data. Individual absence records are also essential for reward schemes and disciplinary processes.

Absence rates are normally calculated as the number of days taken off work excluding annual leave, maternity leave, and authorised absences such as public duty and compassionate leave. Long-term illness beyond a defined length may also be excluded because just one case of several months' duration can distort the general picture. The time remaining after all exclusions is normal certificated and uncertificated sick leave, plus any other unauthorised absence, which can be targeted. Some may argue that certificated sick leave should be excluded because it is unavoidable, but this is too narrow a view – the distinction between avoidable and unavoidable sickness absence is extremely blurred. The absence reduction programme may also include measures to promote healthy living, which may reduce the incidence of what might otherwise have been considered unavoidable sickness.

Comparative or benchmarked data should be examined with care, because there is no standard formula for producing absence indices. Percentages of time lost can be misleading unless the 100 per cent baseline is defined. Is this 288 annual working days, as assumed in the CBI's annual survey, or a different total specific to a particular employer? Are part-timers' absences calculated in terms of hours rather than days? Are half-day absences included? Organisations need to select the types of statistics that best suit their own circumstances, even if they also produce a parallel set of data so that they can take part in standardised surveys such as the CBI's. It may also be useful to monitor the frequency of absences. Ten separate one-day absences may be far more disruptive than two weeks off for a genuine illness. A simple formula is the annual average number of absences per employee.

No absence reduction programme can be effective without the full involvement of line managers. They must

  ensure that all absences, however minor, are recorded

- establish contact with absent staff
- conduct return-to-work interviews.

In many firms, line managers are the only people who know when an employee is absent, particularly when this is for short, uncertificated periods. Computerised recording systems are helpful, both for reducing the work involved in record-keeping and for producing analyses of group and individual attendance, but they may rely for their accuracy on the thoroughness with which supervisors and managers ensure the inputting of minor absence details.

Managers should maintain contact with sick employees, generally by telephoning them from time to time to ask about progress and possible dates of return. This must be handled sensitively, so that individuals are not put under pressure to come back before they are fit. Personnel staff could be asked to take on this task. Some organisations also arrange welfare visits to employees on long-term sick leave.

Return-to-work interviews are probably the most influential element in ensuring that absences are not treated casually. They are particularly important for uncertificated leave. Such interviews are best conducted by an employee's immediate manager, who must be trained to conduct them with the right blend of sensitivity and firm inquiry. The aim is to ask about the reason for an absence, to decide whether the explanation is consistent with other evidence, to address any doubts about its validity, and to identify work-related causes that can be corrected. Where absences are caused by difficult personal circumstances, employees may be referred to the

HR department, the occupational health adviser or other sources of welfare information.

Good attendance can be encouraged by a financial reward, although there may be a danger of promoting the idea that being at work at the correct times is more than a normal requirement. But many firms that give attendance bonuses believe they do reduce absence rates. Bonuses may be paid to individuals, teams or even the whole workforce – the argument for collective bonuses being that they promote group commitment to high levels of attendance. The typical bonus is a quarterly or half-yearly lump sum paid when absences are below a specified level. For group bonuses this may involve a target of, say, 3 or 4 per cent of working time, or possibly a sliding scale of payments related to absence rates.

For individuals, bonuses are usually paid only when the employee has not been absent at all during the period. Deciding the size of a payment requires shrewd judgement. If it is too small, it will have no effect; if it is too large, it may induce sick employees to return before they are fit.

The design of sick-pay schemes must also be addressed because some sickness absence rules can have the opposite effect of that intended. For example, one company which paid for the first day of absence only if it continued for three days or more eventually realised that this encouraged employees to stay away for at least three days. A better approach might be to pay for the first day only if the overall absence rate is kept below a defined level. No type of payment – attendance bonus or sick-pay scheme – is effective on its own. Financial rewards (and the penalty of not being eligible) must be part of an overall approach. Payments need to be seen as a symbol of the importance that the organisation places on good attendance, not as a stand-alone remedy.

Absence can also be reduced by flexible working. Flexi-time schemes that enable people to offset occasional days off by working longer hours on other days may have a significant impact on the time lost on medical and dental appointments. Staff who are job-sharing can arrange for one to cover the other's absence, and there is some evidence that part-timers have lower absence rates than full-time employees. Annual-hours systems operating on a team basis may create peer pressure that reduces absenteeism if staff on standby have to cover for their absent colleagues. Homeworking also enables some people to continue working when they would not otherwise be able to get to their normal workplace.

Other positive measures include the provision of occupational health services, general welfare counselling and the promotion of healthy living. If an organisation is too small to have its own health unit, it may be possible for these services to be provided by a local health centre or hospital. Counselling services can be bought from specialist providers, and their advice on personal concerns should help to reduce stress-related absences. Healthy living programmes may include promoting measures to improve personal fitness, no-smoking policies and providing fitness suites for use outside working hours. Such services do, of course, cost money, but this can be justified if they result in lower absence rates, a more motivated workforce and the reputation of being a good employer.

No effective programme can avoid the issue of disciplinary action. Although the emphasis must be on positive measures that encourage high attendance, people need to understand that exploitation of uncertificated sickness absence will not be tolerated. Any disciplinary action should be based on accurate absence data, in accord with the documented disciplinary procedures and applied consistently across the organisation. An important role for the HR function is to ensure that high standards of fairness and consistency are maintained and to advise individual managers on how best to deal with disciplinary cases. It is also essential that a clear distinction is made between disciplinary action for unacceptable absence and dismissal on medical grounds. The latter requires particularly sensitive handling, partly for obvious personal reasons, but also because of the legal implications of the Disability Discrimination Act 1995.

Further information

1 EVANS A. *and* PALMER S. *From Absence to Attendance.* London, Institute of Personnel and Development, 1997.

2 ADVISORY, CONCILIATION AND ABITRATION SERVICE, *Absence and Labour Turnover.* London, 1994.

Coping with conflict

22   Employee grievances

As with many employment procedures, handling employee grievances requires attention to two issues: relevant employment law, and the wider area of good employment practice. Many organisations barely meet the minimum legislative requirements, and not all see grievance handling as an important element in effective employee management. Yet a procedure which enables grievances to be dealt with promptly and fairly can make a significant contribution to an organisation's reputation as a good employer, and should all but eliminate the adverse effect of unresolved complaints festering within the workforce.

Grievances and the law

The Employment Rights Act 1998 requires that all employees be issued with a written statement of the terms and conditions of their employment. This statement must include a note specifying to whom employees can apply in order to seek redress for any grievances relating to their employment, how this application should be made, and what further steps (if any) they may take after this application. There are several points to note about these provisions, including the fact that they have few teeth. Even if access to a grievance procedure is wrongly denied, there is no direct legal redress for the employee. The law's only requirement is for a grievance mechanism to be notified, although it is arguable that in a serious case an employer's refusal to operate the procedure might justify the employee's leaving and claiming constructive dismissal.

The only legal requirement is for a one-stage process. The employee must know to whom a grievance should be taken. This person can be designated either by name, by job title or by position. There is no requirement to operate a procedure by which an unresolved grievance at one level is referred up the managerial line, although if such a procedure is available the law requires it to be notified to employees. There is a need, however, to state the manner in which grievances must first be raised, not merely to describe the person to whom the grievance should be addressed.

The type of written statement, used by many employers, which says merely that grievances should be addressed to the employee's immediate manager can be faulted for not making clear whether such application should be verbal or in writing, and for not stating whether any time limits apply. So the law provides only a minimal basis for dealing effectively with grievances.

Good employment practice

From a good practice perspective the starting-point is that if an employee feels aggrieved or upset about something, it is best for it to be known, discussed and resolved, and for this process to be completed quickly. This implies a need for more than just a documented procedure. It requires managers to adopt a positive rather than defensive attitude towards grievances, and to see grievance handling as a positive way of identifying and eliminating causes of employee discontent. There is a parallel with the customer complaints procedure. The wise company recognises complaints as a valuable form of quality monitoring. Similarly, knowledge of employees' complaints and concerns is a useful form of monitoring employee morale.

In the absence of a constructive managerial attitude employees may well be reluctant to voice grievances for fear of rebuff, or because of cynicism about the extent to which complaints will be taken seriously. This is not to imply that all grievances are well-founded. Some could be based on misunderstandings about company rules or policies; others may be the result of personality clashes; a few may be deeply felt but irrational.

Furthermore, it is not possible for every grievance to be resolved in the way the employee concerned wishes. Part of the skill in handling grievances effectively is an ability to say no firmly, without any hint of rancour, and with a clear explanation. One of the worst, and unfortunately most common, failings is for a manager to listen to a complaint and consider it unfounded, but, instead of saying so, speaking vaguely about seeing if anything can be done – and then doing nothing.

Stages in the procedure

Except in very small organisations there is a need for more than the simple, one-stage procedure of taking a grievance to the immediate manager. There are likely to be issues which first-line supervisors or managers cannot resolve because they involve matters beyond their knowledge or authority. There may also be cases where the immediate manager is too closely involved to consider the matter objectively – while some grievances may be about the manager's own behaviour. Difficulties of these kinds may be resolved by three further optional stages:

- giving employees who are uncertain how to proceed the opportunity to obtain advice from the relevant personnel officer – the purpose of such advice is primarily to direct the employee into the appropriate channel, not to usurp the role of the manager
- permitting the grievance in the first instance to be taken directly to the next most senior manager if it relates to the conduct of the employee's immediate manager
- providing a confidential counselling contact in cases that involve sensitive personal matters – this might be either a designated personnel officer, who should have had training in this type of counselling, or part of a more general welfare service.

It is important that grievances are dealt with promptly and that employees are not left in a state of suspense, not knowing whether any action is being taken or when they will be told a final decision. The procedure should therefore specify the timescale of each stage, although provision should be left for these to be exceeded if more time is needed to provide an explanation and achieve a resolution.

Finally, there is the matter, referred to in the legislation, of the manner in which a grievance should be raised. There is a balance to be struck here. At one extreme an over-emphasis on informality might give an impression that even the most trivial of complaints will be welcomed and dealt with as a matter of great importance. At the other extreme a highly formal method, requiring the submission of lengthy written statements for even the most minor issues, may deter employees from raising matters which do require managerial attention. Consequently, it may help to make clear to managers and employees that the resolution of employee grievances should be a normal part of everyday, informal managerial action.

Except in unusual and serious circumstances, employees should first talk to their managers about anything of concern. This does not constitute a stage in the formal grievance procedure. The formal procedure, which may then require the submission of a written statement, will start only if the informal approach fails, or if, perhaps after counselling, the employee considers the matter sufficiently serious to warrant such a step.

Grievances relating to disciplinary action, performance assessments, job evaluation and sexual or racial harassment need particularly careful attention. In general, grievances about disciplinary action are best handled within a separate disciplinary procedure. This applies particularly to appeals against dismissal, for which it is necessary, for legal as well as good-practice reasons, to operate a formal appeal process. Occasionally, however, the grievance may be about the manner in which a disciplinary interview or inquiry has been conducted, rather than its outcome. It may then be appropriate to deal with this complaint within the grievance procedure. However, if it is decided that the complaint is well-founded, the best course of action is for the disciplinary issue to be referred back into the disciplinary procedure for a properly conducted reconsideration – not for the grievance procedure to take on a disciplinary role.

A similar principle can be applied to grievances about assessments or job evaluation exercises. The grievance procedure should not be used to challenge the outcome of such processes simply on the grounds that the employee disagrees with the judgements involved. There may, in any event, be a separate appeals procedure for job-grading disputes. What might be acceptable as a genuine grievance is a complaint that the proper procedures for performance or job assessments were not followed – for example, if a manager issued a performance assessment without having first conducted an appraisal interview. As with disciplinary matters, if it is found that proper procedures were not followed, the matter should be referred back for reconsideration within the appropriate procedure.

It may not always be appropriate for grievances about sexual or racial harassment to be dealt with by the employee's immediate manager, although this possibility should not be discouraged if the employee is content to pursue the matter in this way. In other cases, however, access to counselling could prove a more satisfactory initial response. This may be provided by the personnel or equal-opportunities function, or by a welfare counsellor for those organisations which have such a general counselling service.

23 Conciliation and arbitration

Most organisations prefer to resolve disputes with individual employees or trade unions themselves, but situations can arise in which the involvement of an independent third party is beneficial. Circumstances in which this may be a useful course of action include complaints which, in the absence of a mutually acceptable settlement, will be taken to a tribunal, and disputes with trade unions in which negotiation has reached an impasse.

This is not to suggest that third-party intervention should always be used in such cases. There is little point in exploring an out-of-court settlement for unfair dismissal if the employer has a strong case and is not concerned about any publicity which might arise from the employment tribunal hearing. And when breakdown occurs in collective bargaining, sitting out a period of impasse may be an effective tactic. The possible use of external help is a matter of judgement, to be weighed carefully against alternative courses of action.

Before arranging the involvement of a third party it is essential to be clear about its nature, for there are three distinct types of such activity: conciliation, mediation and arbitration.

Conciliation

The conciliator's role is defined by ACAS (the independent Advisory, Conciliation and Arbitration Service) as attempting through discussion and negotiation to enable parties in dispute to reach their own agreements. Conciliators have no power to impose, or even recommend, settlements. They will ensure that there are no misunderstandings between the two parties, will encourage each to think of possible solutions, and may provide factual explanations of, for example, tribunal procedures. They will not try to put pressure on the parties to accept any particular solution. This is of particular importance in cases such as unfair dismissal, over which ACAS has issued firm guidance to its conciliation staff to avoid giving opinions on the merits of a case or recommending particular sums for settlement.

Mediation

A mediator goes further and at the request of the parties will make positive recommendations about a settlement in terms which neither party may have previously considered. There is no commitment in advance to accepting the mediator's proposals, only to giving them serious consideration. Mediation can be particularly useful in a complex collective dispute when the parties themselves think they have exhausted all possible permutations of solutions. An ingenious mediator (perhaps with wider experience of the issues involved) may be able to suggest a wholly new type of settlement package.

Arbitration

The essence of arbitration is that both parties agree in advance to accept whatever solution the arbitrator determines. To win at arbitration depends largely on presenting the arbitrator with a detailed, well-argued case. Each party, in effect, puts its own preferred solution to the arbitrator, who may then either choose one of these or make some alternative award which usually lies somewhere between the two sides' proposals.

Arbitration thus differs fundamentally from conciliation or mediation, for success in those processes requires a readiness to abandon any preconceived solutions. In arbitration, while there has to be an acceptance of the possibility of not obtaining the desired outcome, it is usually embarked on with the objective of convincing the arbitrator that one's own case is to be preferred to the other party's.

Arbitration is rarely used to settle individual employment cases, although it is a common method of settling commercial disputes. If conciliation fails, the employee normally proceeds to a tribunal – the tribunal acting in effect as an arbitrator with the power of legal enforcement. Arbitration is essentially a method of resolving otherwise intractable collective disputes, and it is the ACAS view – and good management practice – that before seeking arbitration efforts should be made to settle a dispute by conciliation or mediation.

ACAS and other third-party assistance

Third-party assistance is particularly useful when the parties in a dispute find it impossible to agree a mutually acceptable solution but both still wish such a solution to be found – implying an acceptance of the possible need for compromise. An independent third party may then be able to help by

- acting as a calming influence on what may have become an overheated disagreement; this enables one or both parties to accept a position which had previously been rejected because it represented a loss of face – but which becomes acceptable when it can be attributed to the advice of a third party
- introducing new ideas, or assisting the two parties in dispute to discover for themselves solutions they had not previously thought of
- acting as a go-between, at least for the initial part of the process, when relationships have deteriorated to a level at which the parties are no longer talking to each other
- reassuring the parties about the legitimacy or good sense of ideas they may previously have rejected.

ACAS is the primary, though not sole, source of independent third-party assistance. Although established by statute, ACAS acts independently of government. There are a number of advantages in using ACAS. It has an outstanding reputation for its skills and impartiality. Its staff have a wealth of experience in achieving settlements in both dismissal and discrimination cases and industrial disputes. There is also the advantage that the confidentiality of matters discussed during an ACAS conciliation in dismissal cases is protected by statute, so nothing can be quoted in any eventual tribunal or court proceedings.

In potential tribunal cases there are two ways in which ACAS may become involved on a conciliation basis, while the 1998 Employment Rights (Disputes Resolution) Act provides for ACAS to establish a scheme of voluntary assistance. For conciliation, one of the parties can approach ACAS for assistance before a complaint has been presented to a tribunal; but this can only happen if there are circumstances in which an entitlement to proceed to tribunal exists – for example, when a dismissal has been effected but the employee has not yet made a formal complaint to an employment tribunal. Either party may also seek ACAS conciliation after a complaint has been registered. ACAS may also become involved when an ACAS officer approaches the parties, offering conciliation services after a formal complaint has been registered. ACAS is notified by tribunal offices of all registered complaints (other than redundancy payment claims), and may then take the initiative in seeking to effect settlements.

Conciliated ACAS settlements are reached in around 60 per cent of all such complaints. It should be noted, however, that there is no statutory obligation on the employee or employer to accept ACAS conciliation, that conciliation cannot take place if one party objects, and that such an objection cannot be quoted against the party concerned in any subsequent legal proceedings.

In collective disputes, particularly those which may be causing public concern, ACAS may take the initiative in offering assistance. More commonly, it is open to either party to seek help from ACAS although, as in individual cases, conciliation can proceed only with the agreement of both parties. Consequently, when trade union negotiations have reached deadlock and a way forward is being sought, it is necessary to seek the union's agreement to ACAS' involvement.

Although ACAS is by far the most widely-used conciliation service, other sources may be worth considering. ACAS statistics suggest that about 20 per cent of all potential employment and discrimination cases are settled out of court without their involvement. While most of these are agreements reached without third-party help, some are made with the aid of non-ACAS conciliators or through solicitors. The most important requirements are that the external facilitator should be accepted by both parties as independent, impartial, and having sufficient knowledge of the issues involved to be credible. Provided they meet these criteria, some possible alternatives to ACAS are:

- non-executive directors
- academics, particularly those working in the fields of business or human resource management
- suitably experienced advice centre staff
- retired managers or trade union officials (or active managers or trade union officers unconnected with the parties to the dispute) who have established a reputation for their integrity and independence in the third-party role
- consultants, although (as with non-executive directors) employees or trade unions may well be unwilling to accept a management-nominated person as sufficiently independent
- jointly nominated solicitors or barristers – ie not a solicitor perceived as acting for either party.

To ensure that any conciliated settlement of a potential tribunal case is legally binding – ie that the case cannot be reopened after acceptance of the settlement terms – it needs to have the status of a 'valid compromise agreement' as defined by the 1998 Employment Act referred to above. This requires the settlement to have been reached with the involvement of a 'relevant independent adviser', who may be

- a solicitor, barrister or authorised advocate or litigator
- trade union officers authorised by their trade union to undertake this conciliation role
- advice centre workers certified as competent to give employment advice.

In resolving collective disputes the two important issues to resolve before resorting to arbitration are the choice of the arbitrator(s) and the terms of reference. If ACAS assistance is sought, the parties to the dispute will be asked to indicate their preference for either a single arbitrator or a panel. If a panel is chosen, it will normally consist of an employer (to whom the employing party must agree), a trade union official (agreed with the trade union party) and an independent person in the chair, normally an academic or a lawyer. If a single arbitrator is chosen, it will require the assent of both parties. ACAS maintains a panel of arbitrators from which these selections can be made.

Agreed terms of reference are then needed to define the parameters of the eventual award. In a pay dispute, for example, these terms must make clear whether it is only the size of a pay award which is to be resolved, or whether the arbitrators may award a package solution which includes other elements. It is also important to specify whether the arbitrators have a free hand in making an award, or whether they are to be asked to support one or other side's proposals (ie pendulum arbitration). ACAS awards are not in themselves legally binding, although in theory they could be made so if the two parties agreed in advance to be bound contractually by them. In the UK such agreements have been exceedingly rare, and arbitration awards are usually treated as binding in honour, not in law.

Further information

1 There are a number of free ACAS publications about the use of conciliation, mediation and arbitration, available from all ACAS regional and area offices.

2 FOWLER A. *Negotiation Skills and Strategies.* 2nd edn. London, Institute of Personnel and Development, 1996.

3 SUTER E. *The Employment Law Checklist.* 6th edn. London, Institute of Personnel and Development, 1997.

4 LEWIS D. *Essentials of Employment Law.* 5th edn. London, Institute of Personnel and Development, 1997.

24   Disciplinary interviews

For many managers, conducting a disciplinary interview can be almost as stressful as it is for the employee concerned. What may have been a pleasant working relationship has to be set aside for a formal event that could lead to serious consequences for the employee – or, if the process is mishandled, severe legal problems for the employer.

Anyone aware of the pitfalls will recognise the need for a fair, calm and systematic approach to an encounter that can too easily become emotional. It is worth remembering that if a disciplinary interview leads to a dismissal that is challenged at an employment tribunal, the way the meeting was conducted may well come under scrutiny as well as the reasons for the dismissal. Any unfairness in this process can result in a finding of unfair dismissal, regardless of the rights or wrongs of the case itself.

The first of many common mistakes is a failure to follow the organisation's formal disciplinary procedure. While statute law does not prescribe what this procedure should be, employees must be given details of the disciplinary rules. If these are not followed, tribunals are likely to find that this failure constitutes unfairness. The most common reason given for bypassing formal procedure is that a case is so obvious that a formal hearing seems unnecessary. The flaw in this argument (apart from the important technicality of failing to comply with the organisation's own rules) is that it is a breach of the principles of natural justice for employees not to be given a chance to hear and respond to complaints made against them.

Three other common mistakes are:

- treating the interview simply as a way of establishing guilt or innocence, ignoring its ability to improve conduct or performance
- failing to distinguish misconduct – for which disciplinary sanctions may be appropriate – from poor performance, which may be the result of poor management
- losing control of the interview by reacting defensively to criticisms made by the employee, and being drawn into an ill-tempered argument.

Whatever the details of the organisation's disciplinary procedure, it should comply with four fundamental criteria:

- The employee must be forewarned of the status of the interview, not simply called in and told, out of the blue, that it is a formal disciplinary hearing.
- The employee must be told in advance what the complaint is, and be given sufficient time to prepare a response.

At the interview the employee must be given an adequate opportunity to provide an explanation.

The employee should have the choice of being accompanied by either a colleague or a union or employee representative.

Preparation for the interview is essential, and a checklist can be used to ensure that nothing has been overlooked:

1 Have all the potential witnesses been interviewed?
2 Are all relevant documents available?
3 Have these documents been copied to the employee?
4 Who will attend the interview
   – to present the management case?
   – to provide witness statements?
   – to take notes?
5 Has the employee been notified of the date, time and location?
6 Has the employee had sufficient time to prepare a response?
7 Has the employee been told of the right to be represented or accompanied?
8 Has the employee notified who will act as his or her representative?
9 Has the employee provided details of his or her witnesses?
10 Is a quiet room available, with telephone calls barred?
11 Has sufficient time been allowed for the interview?

Disciplinary investigations should not be confused with disciplinary interviews. An investigation may involve obtaining statements from witnesses and examining documents such as attendance records. It may result in a decision to take no action, or lead to an informal counselling session. A disciplinary interview will be convened only if the investigation unearths evidence of conduct that may merit disciplinary action. The employer must then decide which parts of the evidence will form the substance of the case, who is to present that case at the interview, and what other witnesses and documentation should be produced.

Although conducting the interview too rigidly might inhibit constructive discussion, there is a greater danger that an unsystematic approach will cause the meeting to degenerate into confusion. Experienced practitioners such as ACAS recommend the following procedure:

1   The complaint against the employee is stated, either by the manager conducting the interview or by someone else deputed to put the management case.
2   Any supporting witnesses make their statements.
3   The employee and his or her representative have the chance to question the manager and witnesses about their statements.
4   The employee (or the representative) gives his or her side of the story and may call supporting witnesses.
5   The manager conducting the interview (or assisting colleagues) questions the employee and the employee's witnesses.
6   There may be a more general discussion in which both sides can raise any issues that were not covered earlier.

7 The employee is given a chance to highlight the aspects he or she wishes to emphasise, including any mitigating circumstances.
8 The manager conducting the interview summarises and adjourns the meeting.
9 During the adjournment the manager considers everything that has come out of the interview and decides what action to take. The length of the adjournment may be quite short in a straightforward case – say, half an hour – or it can be longer if the issues are complex. In all cases the management should avoid jumping, or even appearing to jump, to an immediate conclusion as soon as the interview ends.
10 The meeting is then reconvened and the manager announces the decision. This should then be confirmed in writing.

Adjournments may be necessary in the course of the interview as well as before a decision is made. The employee's response to the complaint may raise unexpected issues that require further analysis. It would be unfair not to make time for this. Tempers may become frayed or the employee may become too emotional for the interview to proceed fairly. In these cases a short break can help to restore calm. It is also not unusual for an interview to take longer than expected. Rushing it to meet a deadline could be viewed as unfair. It is better to adjourn and arrange another time to complete the interview.

The skills required when chairing other kinds of meetings are of value in disciplinary interviews. These include ensuring that everyone understands the purpose and procedure of the interview; keeping control firmly but constructively; preventing progress from becoming slowed by minor matters; ensuring that everyone (particularly the employee) leaves feeling they have said what they wanted to; using adjournments to maximum benefit; and summarising to prevent anyone from misunderstanding the key issues.

Handling an employee's anger skilfully can be very important. Employees charged with a disciplinary offence sometimes respond with personal accusations. Aspersions of this kind can be hurtful, and it is natural to want to refute them. Yet a manager who is provoked into an angry reaction may confirm in the employee's mind the very accusation that has been made. The manager must remain calm and make a reply along the lines of 'I hear what you say, but I am not going to enter into an argument about it. Now let's move on.'

Communication and questioning skills are vital. The employee must understand the issues and their possible consequences. The manager must state key points plainly, repeating them if necessary, and check that they are understood. Communication is a two-way process, and managers must be just as careful to listen as to explain. The questioning skills involved are similar to those in selection interviewing. Open-ended questions should be used, such as 'What happened during the incident involving a customer last Friday?' rather than closed or leading questions such as 'Were you rude to a customer last Friday?' Managers also must avoid any line of questioning that could be seen as indicating a discriminatory attitude towards women, the disabled or people from ethnic minorities.

Counselling skills may also be relevant. Even when disciplinary action is fully justified, there are often cases where it can be combined with counselling. The best outcome of many disciplinary interviews is that the employee remains in employment and improves his or her conduct or performance. To achieve this, the manager may need to encourage the employee to see why faults have occurred and suggest improvements.

So instead of saying 'If you are late without good reason more than twice in the next three months, you will be dismissed,' the counselling approach would be 'Because you are now on a final warning, I think you should set yourself a timekeeping target. What do you think you should aim for over, say, the next three months?' An improvement target 'owned' by an employee is far more likely to be met than one imposed without discussion.

Further information

FOWLER A. *The Disciplinary Interview*. London, Institute of Personnel and Development, 1996.

25 Preparing an employment tribunal case

Thorough preparation is essential to achieving a satisfactory outcome in an employment tribunal case. (Industrial Tribunals were renamed Employment Tribunals by the 1998 Employment Rights (Disputes Resolution) Act.) Although tribunals are conducted less formally than the main courts, it is necessary to understand their procedures and preferences in the way cases are presented. Basically sound cases are sometimes damaged by the employer's falling foul of some element of tribunal practice, or failing to prepare for possible arguments to be used by the other party.

This article uses unfair dismissal to exemplify the issues, but similar principles apply to the preparation of other types of cases. Seven aspects are particularly important:

- assessing the strong and weak points of the case
- completing the IT3 form
- producing the bundle of documents
- selecting and counselling the witnesses

- planning the content and sequence of the presentation of the case
- planning the cross-examination
- identifying relevant case law.

Assessing the case

A thorough assessment of the strong and weak points of the case is an essential precursor to all subsequent action, not least because it may lead to a decision to seek a settlement rather than contest the case. The case should be examined not only from the employer's viewpoint but from that of the tribunal and of a skilled advocate for the other party. A valuable role for the personnel manager to play is that of devil's advocate, talking to the managers involved in the dismissal and probing their explanations for weak points. Managers who object should be reminded that if they are to be witnesses at the tribunal, they will be subjected to just such cross-examination by the other party. Far better to discover flaws in the privacy of the office than publicly at the tribunal.

It is important to understand that tribunals follow a standard sequence of questions in reaching their decision, to which clear, convincing answers are necessary. These are:

- What was the reason, or principal reason, for the dismissal?
- Is this one of the acceptable reasons listed in the legislation?
- Did the employer act reasonably, all things considered, in treating the reason as sufficient to justify dismissal?

■ If the dismissal was for misconduct, did the employer genuinely believe the employee was culpable, and was this belief reasonable in the light of the results of an adequate investigation?

■ Was the dismissal procedure fair?

■ Did the dismissal lie within a band of reasonable possible responses by the employer?

The outcome of this review may be a decision to seek a settlement, or to proceed to a full tribunal hearing, or, if the employee's case is extremely weak, to seek a pre-hearing assessment in the hope that the tribunal will warn the employee of the risks of proceeding.

The IT3

The first formal step for a normal hearing is to respond to the official notification of a complaint, form IT2, by completing form IT3, known as the notice of appearance. This is sent to the employer by the tribunal office, together with a copy of IT1, the employee's originating application. The IT3 asks for sufficient details to show the grounds on which you intend to resist the application. While this does not require a lengthy explanation of the case, it is advisable to provide a very clear statement of the reason for the dismissal and why this was considered reasonable grounds for dismissal. Brief references to previous warnings, to the fact that a thorough investigation was held and to any appeal hearings are all useful points to make at this stage. There are situations in which alternatives may need to be put. For example, the fact of dismissal may be disputed. In this case, the IT3 entry should say that no dismissal occurred, but if dismissal is found, then it was fair. The completed IT3 must be returned to the IT office not later than 14 days after its initial receipt by the employer.

The employee's statement (IT1) may fail sufficiently to explain the nature of the complaint, making it difficult to respond adequately on the IT3. It is then possible to write to the tribunal office seeking an order requiring the employee to provide 'further and better particulars'.

The bundle of documents

Although tribunal hearings are concerned primarily with the questioning of witnesses, documentary evidence can be of great importance. For example, an entry in a manager's work diary of a verbal warning given to an employee will add credibility to the manager's verbal evidence.

All relevant documents should be assembled into what lawyers term 'a bundle'. This should consist of all the documents to be used at the hearing, in the order they will be referred to, with consecutive page numbers written prominently at the top right-hand corner for easy reference. At least one original and five copies are needed: three for the tribunal, one for the other party, and one for the witness table. It is permissible to include documents whose authors will not be called to give evidence, but all such material must be sent to the IT office and the other party at least seven days before the hearing.

In practice, it is best to send the whole bundle to the IT office and the other party well in advance of the hearing. Form IT4, the notification of the hearing date, also suggests that the parties might agree a single consolidated bundle, although this is not essential or always practicable.

The bundle can be used to let the tribunal members see material which may influence their view of the case, whether or not the documents actually figure in the hearing. For example, a copy of an employee's employment history which shows very frequent job changes may be included with the contract documents, even if in the event it is not actually referred to directly by any of the witnesses. Essential documents to include in any dismissal case include the contract of employment, a copy of the disciplinary procedure, records of any disciplinary investigation, disciplinary hearing and appeal hearing, copies of any previous written warnings or recorded verbal warnings, and a copy of the employee's dismissal letter.

Witnesses

The choice of witnesses to give evidence is a matter for decision by each party. The tribunal itself cannot require a witness to be called. Either party may ask for an order to make an unwilling witness attend, but tribunals will not grant such orders when it seems that the witness will be hostile.

There is no legal requirement to call all the people involved in the case. It is certainly risky to call, say, a manager who disagreed with the decision to dismiss, even though he or she was directly involved in the disciplinary investigation. Under cross-examination this management disagreement might be revealed and weaken the case. Nevertheless, tribunals prefer to hear directly from the principal actors rather than learning about them from the person presenting the case. There is an opposite fault: calling more witnesses than is necessary to establish the key features of the case. Tribunals are irritated by a procession of witnesses who add only peripheral information.

Witnesses should have the IT procedure explained to them, be advised about the evidence they will be asked to give, and be given practice in answering the awkward questions which they may be asked during cross-examination or by tribunal members. This briefing should stop short of learning answers by rote or, of course, of being untruthful. Witnesses should be counselled to respond concisely only to the questions they are asked, and not to add their own comments. The more they say, the wider and less predictable will be their cross-examination. Witnesses are not normally allowed to refer to guidance notes – only to their own documents or records which are contemporary with the incidents to which they refer.

Content and sequence

There is a temptation to provide evidence about anything detrimental to the other party, even though the relevance to the case in question is remote. This is dangerous. It may give an impression of vindictiveness and open the door to cross-examination on a much wider front than is desirable.

The sequence in which the employer's case is set out is also important. In most cases it is best presented as a chronological account, starting with the employee's original appointment, progressing through relevant parts of the employment history (such as previous warnings) to the incidents which led to dismissal, and finishing with an account of the dismissal process.

In presenting a case there is no requirement to make an opening statement, but it may be helpful to prepare a brief summary and ask the tribunal for permission to make it. This should do no more than explain the central points of the employer's case, and say which witnesses will be called in what order. However, tribunal chairmen do not always permit such statements and, instead, ask whoever is presenting the case to begin immediately by calling the first witness. A concise closing statement is more important as both parties are always given the opportunity of a final summing-up. This can be partly prepared in advance, but will need to deal with other matters raised during the hearing.

Cross-examination

Cross-examination of the other party's witnesses can be a vital part of the procedure but cannot be wholly prepared in advance. Much will depend on what the witnesses say in evidence. But it is possible before the hearing to identify key issues on which a challenge to the other party's evidence can be made.

It is worth remembering that questions do not have to be limited to what the witness has said, so some can be prepared in advance to cover points adverse to the other party's case. It is also permissible to ask questions which undermine the witness's credibility and to ask leading questions in cross-examination. Be wary, however, of asking questions without having any clue about the possible answers.

Relevant case law

In the final summing-up it is often helpful to quote relevant case law, although this should not be overdone: tribunals do not need to be lectured about leading cases – it may help simply to mention them to show the employer is aware of them and has followed these precedents. There are instances, however, where direct references to less well-known cases can help the tribunal focus on the key issues. If so, tribunal chairmen appreciate advance notice of the references being used. This can be done informally by giving a note to the tribunal clerk just before the hearing begins. The relevant law reports can then be made available for the tribunal's eventual deliberations.

Further information

1 GREENHALGH R. *Industrial Tribunals*. London, Institute of Personnel and Development, 1995.

2 INCOMES DATA SERVICES. *Industrial Tribunal Practice and Procedure*. London, 1994.

With over 90,000 members, the **Institute of Personnel and Development** is the largest organisation in Europe dealing with the management and development of people. The IPD operates its own publishing unit, producing books and research reports for human resource practitioners, students, and general managers charged with people management responsibilities.

Currently there are nearly 200 titles covering the full range of personnel and development issues. The books have been commissioned from leading experts in the field and are packed with the latest information and guidance to best practice.

For free copies of the IPD Books Catalogue, please contact the publishing department:

Tel.: 0181–263 3387
Fax: 0181–263 3850
E-mail: publish@ipd.co.uk
Web: http://www.ipd.co.uk

Orders for books should be sent to:

Plymbridge Distributors
Estover
Plymouth
Devon
PL6 7PZ

(Credit card orders) Tel.: 01752 202 301
Fax: 01752 202 333

Get More – and More Value – from Your People
Alan Fowler

Today, organisations have to maximise the value that they get from each and every employee. Although this is partly a question of leadership, it is also about creating robust yet flexible structures that support staff effectiveness.

Alan Fowler's articles in the IPD's fortnightly magazine *People Management* have long been established as a definitive source of guidance. The best of these articles have now been collected in two companion volumes and published alongside the invaluable suggestions for employees to be found in Neasa Mac-Erlean's *Get More from Work – and More Fun.*

The present book examines:

- getting the right people on board: from recruitment advertising or executive search to interviews and induction
- signing them up: standard and innovative forms of employment contract
- putting together the reward package: from basic salary structures to flexible benefits, childcare services and company cars
- enhancing the skills base: identifying training needs, choosing methods to meet them and evaluating the results.

Not every organisation can afford a large personnel department, but all can learn to apply the basic principles of good practice. They are clearly summarised in this invaluable volume.

1998   208 pages   0 85292 747 9   **£9.95**

Get More from Work –
and More Fun
Neasa MacErlean

Neasa MacErlean's hugely successful 'How To' columns in the *Observer* have long been an invaluable source of help for all those getting to grips with the world of work or seeking better prospects. Over 100 of these columns have now been collected into a single volume.

The book examines (among many other topics):

- CV-writing
- preparing for psychological tests
- asserting yourself
- negotiating a pay rise
- keeping up with office gossip
- avoiding stress
- changing jobs
- networking
- resigning.

1998   224 pages   0 85292 750 9   **£9.95**